SHOGUN
MANAGEMENT™

SHOGUN MANAGEMENT™

HOW NORTH AMERICANS CAN
THRIVE IN JAPANESE COMPANIES

WILLIAM C. BYHAM, Ph.D.

with George Dixon

HarperBusiness
A Division of HarperCollinsPublishers

A hardcover edition of this book was published in 1993 by HarperBusiness, a division of HarperCollins Publishers.

First paperback edition published 1994.

Designed by Irving Perkins Associates

The Library of Congress has catalogued the hardcover edition as follows:

Byham, William C.
    Shogun management : how North Americans can thrive in Japanese companies /
    William C. Byham with George Dixon. — 1st ed.
        p.   cm.
    Includes bibliographical references and index.
    ISBN 0-88730-630-6
    1. Industrial management—Japan. 2. Industrial management—North America.
3. Corporations, Japanese—North America. 4. Corporate culture—Japan.
5. Corporate culture—North America. I. Dixon, George, 1952–   . II. Title.
HD70.J3B93   1993
658´.00973—dc20   92-54747

ISBN 0-88730-688-8 (pbk.)

94   95   96   97   98   CW   10   9   8   7   6   5   4   3   2   1

To Mrs. Miyo Umeshima, president of Management Service Center Company, Ltd., of Japan, who not only has been a dear friend for twenty-two years but has helped me to learn, understand, and respect both the culture and the people of Japan.

CONTENTS

PART THREE

DEVELOPING THE JAPANESE ORGANIZATION IN NORTH AMERICA

PART FOUR

SHARED RESPONSIBILITY FOR DEVELOPING INDIVIDUALS AND THE ORGANIZATION

ACKNOWLEDGMENTS

GEORGE DIXON CONDUCTED many interviews with Japanese and American managers and participated, as a full partner, in the writing and editing of this book. He not only improved the writing of others but he also contributed many personal insights as he guided the overall development of the book. Without him, *Shogun Management*™ would not exist.

Noriko Yagi and Ku Tashiro extensively critiqued the final draft and provided important first-person insights into Japanese management principles and practices. Mari Kato O'Connell verified the accuracy of all Japanese terminology used in the book, and provided phonetic spelling for all terms used.

Many associates from Development Dimensions International also made important contributions by critiquing various drafts and offering ideas; others worked diligently on the production of the book. Individuals who deserve special recognition include Shelby Gracey, Mary Holden, Sandy Howell, Linda Kapustynski, Anne Maers, Billie Nestor, Matt O'Connell, Carol Schuetz, Kathy Shomo, and Mary Jo Sonntag. Other DDI associates who assisted with *Shogun Management*™ include Michele Bradac, David Cohen, Chuck Cosentino, Darla Cronin, Andrea Eger, Nena Frederick, John Hayden, Bill Jackson, Ruth Jones, Helene Lautman, Bob Matzen, Marcia Medvid, Dyan Moorhead, Cindi Olson, Mary Szpak, and Debra Walker. The book cover was designed by Pam A. Miller and Stacy Rae Zappi.

INTRODUCTION

AFTER THE HONEYMOON

People say you're crazy to work for a Japanese company, but the way I see it, this is the best thing going for me right now and I intend to stick it out.

AMERICAN ENGINEER

Japanese labor relations differ from ours in many ways that look like mistakes to American eyes. . . . All in all, economists weaned on Western economic thought must conclude that Japan does almost everything wrong. Such a litany of errors should cost them dearly. Yet Japan's economy is a dynamo. How do they do it?

PRINCETON PROFESSOR

Japanese companies do very well in the United States—but they could do a lot better if they could just learn how to handle people.

AN AMERICAN PRESIDENT OF A
JAPANESE BANK

BEFORE THE 1980s, few Japanese wondered what it would be like to work in North America. They gave little thought to dealing with North Americans as managers and colleagues, living in the same neighborhoods, or shopping in the same stores. Even as the Japanese economy began to extend its global reach, few wondered about how the new multinational Japanese company would differ from the old model. What would it be like working with North Americans? To Japanese managers and production employees alike, the question was largely irrelevant.

The question was just as irrelevant in North America. Before the eighties began, the Japanese-owned and -managed company in North America was an object of little more than local curiosity—like the occasional sushi bar found in a few large North American cities or the subcompact Japanese cars sometimes sighted on the road. What would it be like to work with Japanese in a Japanese company? Different, probably, but since a career in a Japanese company was a prospect few North Americans contemplated, few really cared.

The indifference has long since evaporated. During the 1970s, the number of Americans working for Japanese companies never rose much beyond 65,000. By 1990, it had risen to nearly 400,000 at more than 1,000 Japanese facilities in forty-five of the fifty U.S. states. By the end of the 1990s, according to projections, more than one million U.S. and Canadian citizens will be employed in Japanese companies. Countless millions more will work for suppliers and service companies that depend on Japanese companies for the bulk of their business.

The burgeoning presence of Japanese companies in North America is an economic experiment on a historically unmatched scale. In fact, the conditions Japanese companies encounter in the United States and Canada might be unique in economic history. The United States still possesses the largest and, in many ways, most productive economy in the world. Its gross national product is still twice that of Japan's. Its business culture is highly developed and mature. The work habits of its citizens are fairly entrenched, and its employment laws and regulations are among the most complex and comprehensive of any nation. Significantly, the majority of its millions of workers are educated and proud—with clear expectations about the roles and relationships of employers and employees.

So far, the Japanese experience in North America, despite some tumultuous moments, has been characterized as a "honeymoon." Supposedly, during this period, each side has made maximum allowances for the strange and sometimes unsettling behavior of their foreign partners. Now, however, the honeymoon is ending. A new phase has begun in which Japanese and North Americans are getting down to business and settling into a predictable and routine pattern of working together.

In this book we explore evidence suggesting that the marriage is beginning to sour. Disenchantment is growing among North Americans trying to stake out a future with Japanese companies. Various surveys and polls conducted in North America show that the majority of local supervisors and managers employed by Japanese organizations feel dissatisfied and often *betrayed* by what they've encountered in Japanese organizations. The adjustment process is proving far tougher than many ever anticipated. The purpose of this book is to explore the causes and the extent of this disenchantment and to suggest ways that Japanese and North American managers can adjust to one another. Our hope is that the mutual expectations of both sides can be satisfied.

THE ORGANIZATION THAT REFUSES TO BLEND

For the most part, Japanese companies have tried to be sensitive to the feelings of North American managers and employees. By necessity, Japanese companies have undertaken a crash course in creating the global business cultures that U.S. and European companies have had decades to develop. Their aim, many Japanese companies say, is the creation of a "blended" business environment in North America—a "third-culture" organization that combines the strengths of the world's two foremost business cultures. The result is intended to be a new and revolutionary type of industrial organization.

The Japanese contribution to this blended organization includes uniquely effective organizational skills, unsurpassed manufacturing methods, an unrelenting focus on customer needs and wants, and above all, the capital to fund new facilities and create jobs. The North American contribution, while more difficult to define, includes marketing skills; creativity; research and development expertise; an aggressive, innovative, and risk-taking management style; and an educated, experienced, and ambitious work force.

Like many others who have been following the evolving Japanese-North American business partnership, we believe that this collaborative, blended organization offers the best hope for the long-term success of Japanese organizations in North America. Many Japanese companies have made progress on the long road toward building a blended organization. But numerous others, as we intend to show, mostly through the voices and experiences of North Americans employed by Japanese companies, have made only fitful progress and, in some cases, so little progress that mounting problems threaten to erase much of what they have already achieved in North America.

A MODERN SHOGUNATE?

The reasons for the lack of progress of many Japanese companies in North America are complex. Part of the explanation can be found in the words of one American manager, who has adopted the terminology of Japan's feudal Shogun period. He describes his Japanese colleagues as "samurai." He and his fellow Americans are "vassals" and powerless "foot soldiers." His company is run by a faceless, collegial "shogunate" in Tokyo practicing ironfisted remote control by telephone and facsimile machine. The "system," as this American defines it, is highly centralized. The hierarchies within it are composed of strictly defined social classes with little mobility between them. The unseen shogunate makes mysterious decisions and communicates them secretly to the samurai administrators on the scene. At the bottom of the heap are the Americans, many of whom are professionals and managers. It is a strange, new predicament for them, and many are deeply resentful.

To some Americans, the analogy might seem strained; to others, it is perfectly apt. Based on our experiences, we think the latter category of Americans is growing. Indeed, the Japanese organization in North America *can* seem like a feudal shogunate. Japanese companies are perceived as being unable and unwilling to give up control. The decision-making process is seen as rigid, secret, and jealously guarded. Despite attractive salaries and recruiting promises, North Americans often see their roles as largely symbolic—as "window dressing" to make the growing Japanese presence in North America more palatable. Promises of career advancement and opportunities to eventually join the ranks of decision makers have not been kept. A "*gaijin* (gai-jēēn) ceiling" keeps local managers permanently stuck in their current positions.

Views of this "shogunate" differ by organizational level. At the employee and lower-supervisory level, North Americans often find the differences they encounter to be refreshing and exciting. With their participatory style and their respect for "voices from below," Japanese companies impress and challenge nonmanagement employees accustomed to merely following orders. At the supervisory level, a different picture emerges. Although supervisors appreciate the openness and increased participation as much as production employees do, they often report confusion about their authority and roles in the Japanese organizations.

The real problems emerge with North American managers and executives. For many of the reasons described in this book, communication and trust between North American and Japanese managers often do not exist. Although both groups operate on parallel tracks, only the North Americans are forced to conclude that their track leads nowhere. This lack of management integration has led to losses in productivity and errors in planning. Language barriers, pride, a lack of trust, miscommunication, and miscomprehension play a part in the mistakes being made. And these mistakes are not easy to undo.

We know of one Japanese firm that is suffering extremely high employee turnover three years after a series of management actions were taken that the local community viewed as inappropriate. Today, the company is still perceived as one that reneges on its promises. Few in the local community trust it. Even with relatively high local unemployment rates, the firm has trouble finding qualified applicants. Here and in other places, we see that when relations between North Americans and their Japanese employers sour, demoralization can spread quickly. When Japanese organizations start off with mistrust and misunderstanding, personnel problems may prove persistent, no matter how hard these organizations try to reverse their initial mistakes.

There are numerous lessons to learn from the Japanese experience in North America. Those lessons are what this book is about. Our purpose is to help Japanese managers and North American employees at all levels efficiently create a blended culture. Our message is that both sides need to change. Change, of course, is never easy. In the special situation in which North Americans and Japanese find themselves, change runs up against the formidable barriers of confusion and mistrust. Removing those barriers will take far more empathy, patience, and training—on both sides—than Japanese and North Americans generally realize.

A WORD ABOUT THE BACKGROUND OF THIS BOOK

The author and his colleagues at Development Dimensions International, Inc., have had years of experience consulting with Japanese companies in Japan and in North America. We are proud to have close, ongoing "partnership" relationships with a significant number of major Japanese employers. Many of these organizations have served as positive models of innovative and effective management of North Americans.

Shogun Management™ is written out of a desire to help our Japanese and North American colleagues avoid the traps described in this book. Both sides should benefit from reading this book. Japanese managers will gain a heightened awareness of the feelings and frustrations of their North American counterparts and the Japanese managers' role relative to those feelings. North American employees, supervisors, and managers will develop insights into what's in store for them when they join a Japanese organization. Few North Americans now have a genuine appreciation for life inside a Japanese organization in North America. And few know how to make the best of the opportunity afforded them by working for a Japanese company.

Readers will note quickly that very few names appear in this book. Many may tire of reading "says one North American manager" or "says one Japanese manager." But the reason for the anonymity is practical: To encourage people to describe their experiences and feelings as openly as possible, we promised not to identify individuals or companies. Where we have used company names, we have either obtained permission or drawn the information from public sources such as articles or speeches.

More than 200 Canadian and U.S. managers working for Japanese companies and a smaller number of Japanese managers were interviewed for this book. Their experiences are presented anonymously but accurately. In addition, we had access to several company-sponsored surveys of Japanese and North American managers that dealt with issues of intercultural communication, adjustment, and cooperation. These surveys were completed by employees of American companies operating in Japan and by employees of Japanese companies operating in North America.

Our research took us to every part of the United States and Canada and into every type of organization, from manufacturing to administrative to financial to communication. We found numerous Japanese organizations that are thriving. However, we believe we discovered common patterns and experiences that are causing problems at the majority of Japanese organizations. The purpose of this book is to examine these patterns and experiences—and to consider what to do about them.

APPLICATION TO JAPANESE ORGANIZATIONS IN MEXICO, EUROPE, AND SOUTHEAST ASIA

Early drafts of the manuscript were based on information obtained from Japanese and local managers in the United States and Canada. After this book was substantially completed, we had the opportunity to interview local managers and employees in five Japanese organizations in Mexico and several dozen organizations in Europe and Southeast Asia. Their experiences, satisfactions, and frustrations were strikingly similar to those reported by North Americans. While we recognize the limitation of our sample, we believe that the insights and suggestions provided in this book are appropriate for most Japanese overseas operations—not just for Japanese organizations in North America.

PART ONE

JAPANESE
AND
NORTH AMERICANS
TOGETHER

1

WINDOW DRESSING

No one buys into this enterprise. Everyone feels isolated and mistrustful. We're just waiting for the opportunity to take what we've learned here—and we've learned a lot—and move on to a company we can feel a part of. It's a shame, too, because this place started out with such a bang.

AMERICAN MANAGER

THESE WORDS COME from a middle-aged American manager who has been working for a Japanese company for two years. The company is known throughout the world for products ranging from robots to construction equipment. Its Midwestern plant, where this American works, is one of the company's largest investments outside of Japan. The company's objectives are suggested by the mission statement for the company's North American operation, which is presented in press releases and bronze letters on a wall in the lobby of the plant, and reads, in part, "A Global Company That Harmonizes the Best of Japan and America to Build Better Lives for Everyone."

The statement is meant to describe an ideal organization that combines Japan's peerless production techniques and relentless organizational efficiency with American management and marketing expertise. In some ways, that ambitious goal has been realized. In

3

other ways, as the American manager's dissatisfaction shows, the company's efforts have stalled, and little progress appears likely in the years ahead.

The company invested heavily in recruiting production employees, and the efforts paid off handsomely. Many American employers hire high school graduates for production jobs because they believe that more schooling might result in workers being overqualified for the monotonous assembly-line routine of traditional North American production environments. This Japanese company, however, wanted production workers who were several cuts above typical American standards. Its production system is based on continuous productivity improvement initiatives suggested and implemented by production workers. That required workers with a solid "basic" education (actually advanced by American standards). In addition, applicants were screened for their problem-solving abilities and enthusiasm for working as team members. They completed a full day of assessment, and only a fraction were offered jobs. The goal was to build a work force close in spirit and attitude to Japanese workers.

Less attention was paid to recruiting American managers. With a tight start-up timetable, the company needed local managers who had experience in similar production environments, as well as strong people-management skills. The fluid North American job market provided plenty of candidates, so it was easy to attract well-qualified and aggressive North American managers with the help of an executive recruiting firm. These new managers came ready and willing, so they said, to abandon some of their ingrained notions about the way industrial organizations are supposed to operate. They looked forward, they told their new Japanese colleagues, to the chance to get in on the "ground floor" of the manufacturing organization of the future. They said they knew they had months, maybe years, of watching, listening, and learning before they could equal their Japanese counterparts' expertise in production methods and organizational techniques.

Some of the potential difficulties facing the new operation were easy for both the Americans and the Japanese to foresee. For example, both sides knew that communicating would be a challenge. Together they agreed on ground rules designed to make the flow of information easier and more natural. The Japanese would have to bear most of the communication burden, at least in the early days; and, despite their limited English-speaking abilities, the Japanese pledged to use English as much as possible. They also agreed that no meetings were to be held in which attendance was restricted to Japanese participants.

Other ground rules were designed to make the American managers partners with the Japanese—if not partners in final decisions, at the very least partners in sharing data, ideas, and planning responsibilities. For a while that goal seemed realistic, although problems cropped up early. Meetings were difficult, of course, given the language barriers. The Japanese had to stop frequently and discuss things among themselves in Japanese to make sure they understood the Americans correctly. The Americans, used to arguing forcefully for their ideas, realized they had to back off frequently, because any hint of conflict made the Japanese uncomfortable. Occasionally, some Japanese managers would nod off during meetings, which the Americans attributed to overwork, to lack of sleep, and to the surprising fact that sleeping during meetings is acceptable to the Japanese.

Some of the Americans also were surprised by the naiveté of the Japanese managers regarding North American employment practices. Japanese managers frequently wanted to reject applicants for reasons the Americans knew could lead to missing some outstanding people, in addition to creating the possibility of expensive legal battles and poor public relations. The Japanese, however, quickly learned to rely on the judgment of the American personnel director, and acknowledged their lack of experience, their desire to learn, and their intention to be good corporate citizens. On that front, the plant eventually became a huge success by local standards, with better ratios of minorities than any other plant in the area.

But progress toward integrated decision making among American and Japanese managers, which was always held out as a promise, never materialized. For one thing, the sheer difficulty of communicating made it easy to waive the "no Japanese only" meeting rule, and increasingly, Japanese managers began meeting among themselves. Soon, the Americans felt they were locked out of the decision-making process altogether, as policies began changing without their input. On one occasion, a new production target was set by headquarters in Tokyo, but was not communicated to the American managers in the manufacturing operation for weeks. They did not know the goals had changed until they were informed that Tokyo was unhappy with their performance.

Eventually, some of the Americans concluded that the real business of running the company was taking place after-hours in meetings among the Japanese in local restaurants. Information was filtered back to the Americans on a highly selective basis, often in the form of new decisions that were the opposite of decisions the Americans thought had been reached the previous day in a joint meeting with the Japanese.

The experiences of an American production manager seem to be typical. One thing this American thought he had learned in twenty-five years of experience in similar American production environments was how to run a production operation. The new Japanese facility, however, sometimes made him feel that he didn't know anything at all. The weeks he spent at the parent operation in Japan after he was hired made him realize just how much the Japanese had refined the production process; how every employee, every detail, every step seemed to contribute to high quality and low cost. When it came to the ability to make products, the Japanese seemed to have vaulted so far ahead of other nations that the American wondered how his country could ever catch up. In fact, he wondered if this type of "partnership" between Americans and Japanese might not be the only way to rejuvenate American industry.

Although the American was never told that some day he would have the chance to run the operation, he felt the message was implied in everything his new employer said to him. The scenario would unfold like this: Once he mastered the production methods of his new employer and the management philosophy—and demonstrated he could handle the difficult task of adapting *them* to an American environment without diluting their Japanese strengths—he would be given increasing responsibility for production. Eventually, he would become the senior executive in charge of operations. No timetable was specified, but he had been promised—as had all the Americans—that eventually the company would become an "American" company, albeit one with a strong Japanese heritage, run mostly by Americans.

Implicit in that promise was the opportunity to advance to whatever level an individual's skills and performance allowed. But more and more, this manager, like others, came to feel that little personal progress was possible. The longer the plant operated, the greater the feeling became. In one week, for instance, the American's Japanese coordinator—his "partner" in the enterprise—had several visitors from Japan. They spent days poring over operations, asking questions, taking notes, pulling people out of production meetings and off the line. Something was going on, and the American figured he had a right to know what it was. After all, his knowledge of the production system was by now so complete that he could have sketched the mechanical system in his sleep. If something needed improvement, he could help. If something wasn't working, he was willing to take the blame. But his coordinator refused to tell him who the visitors were or the nature of their mission. "It doesn't really concern you," his coordinator insisted. "Stop being so paranoid."

He and his coordinator had spent a lot of time together. Initially they had been wary of each other; their relationship was polite and superficial. They circled around each other in a shy kind of courtship. Soon, however, both began to form a grudging respect for each other—grudging because of the different ways they saw the world and did things. Both figured there were things about the other they'd probably never understand.

The language barrier made developing a true friendship difficult, as did the indirect way the American discovered he had to make requests and suggestions. Although they were supposed to be a team, the American often found he needed an intermediary to sound out ideas, and often he would not know if the message had gotten through the way he had intended. He knew he couldn't be blunt. If he discovered a problem, he had to present it carefully—vaguely at first, and then, depending on his coordinator's reaction, in more specific terms. It made communication difficult; and because the two were supposed to share information constantly, it caused several production problems and missed deadlines that could have been avoided.

For all these reasons, a cohesive Japanese-North American management team never really formed. Instead of being integrated into the decision-making process, the Americans grew increasingly estranged from it. Both sides seemed to try to be sensitive to their foreign counterparts, but the gap never narrowed. Lack of progress led the Americans, impatient for change, to wonder why they were hired in the first place. Were they intended to serve as "window dressing"—an American front for an operation that never intended to be anything other than Japanese?

Aware of the feeling, and sharing it himself, the American personnel director has tried to attack the problem several times by getting the American and Japanese managers together at weekend retreats. The liquor and the emotions flow freely at such events, providing a kind of catharsis for the frustrations both sides feel. The problems that evolve from the discussion follow a pattern: The Americans plead for more information, clearer goals and expectations, more career progress, and unambiguous and direct feedback; the Japanese ask the Americans to be better team players and more understanding of the unusual nature of the enterprise. The message from the Japanese is to accept the situation. The message from the Americans is that the situation is unacceptable. Nonetheless, after each retreat, managers on both sides vow to push harder to make the operation work. Within days, however, things usually return to normal. "By Wednesday, it's as if the meetings had never happened," says the American personnel director. "It's almost heartbreaking to see how hard the Japanese try sometimes. I know this is tough and stressful for them, but things just aren't getting better—for us or them."

Not surprisingly, the operation has an uncomfortably high turnover rate among American managers. In fact, most of the original American managers have left. New American managers are hired, but the process is disruptive. Production employees, despite their intelligence and unusual aptitude, haven't managed to reach the level of productivity the company originally anticipated, due largely to the continuously changing layer of supervisors and middle managers above them, which has had a negative impact on their morale and confidence in the company. They remain hesitant to make suggestions and take initiative because of the uncertainty over who is in charge. At the top of the company, senior Japanese managers are rotated back to Tokyo every two or three years. The frequent reassignments are part of their development process; and, besides, no one wants to stay in America too long and risk losing touch with important people back home. The reception back home is often less than enthusiastic, however, because the American operation never met production or quality targets or lived up to original financial projections. Such failure is very hard for Japanese managers to live down.

ADVISORS/COORDINATORS

Advisors (also called shadow managers and coordinators) are a unique feature of Japanese operations outside Japan. They are paired, one to one, with North American managers. Their job is to act as a coordinating link between the Japanese parent company and the subsidiary. They advise and consult with their assigned American manager and supposedly work only through him or her. However, it will be noted in this book that there are many exceptions to this. Many North Americans feel that, because of their access to Japan, coordinators and advisors control the real power. In fact, one American manager explained it this way: "If my American boss tells me one thing, and the Japanese advisor tells me something else, I always do what the advisor says to do. I know who controls promotions."

2

THE FLEXIBLE/INFLEXIBLE

JAPANESE MANAGER

Japanese managers seem to be a study in contradiction. They are at times humble and at times arrogant. Their management skills sometimes seem supernaturally effective and sometimes surprisingly awkward. Their views on human resources practices are both flexible and rigid. You just can't pin them down.

AMERICAN MANAGER IN
CALIFORNIA

The investment spurt has been so sudden that Japanese companies have an acute shortage of executives who can operate in a foreign country. They need more people who can handle the complexities of a multinational work force, labor unions, lawsuits, and cultural gaps. The problem is especially severe at the level just below the top—the level of the "general managers," usually in their 40s, who are the linchpin of international operations at most Japanese companies.

Wall Street Journal,
JANUARY 14, 1987

READY OR NOT

WHAT STRENGTHS DO Japanese *kachos* (kă-chōs), managers just below the top, bring to the North American workplace? Do their experiences in Japan prepare them to confront the very different set of challenges they encounter in North America?

These questions are critically important to Japanese companies. Because the scale of Japanese global operations has grown so dramatically, and because many Japanese companies have only limited numbers of overseas "specialists," the burden of making Japanese investments in overseas operations successful has often fallen on section chiefs, work group managers, and other middle managers whose experiences rarely extend beyond Japan's borders. Of course, the challenge of finding qualified managers to staff overseas assignments is not unique to Japanese companies; American and European organizations face similar problems.

The American problem is compounded by the fact that foreign language study is virtually ignored by many U.S. students. This creates the challenge of finding managers who have the technical expertise as well as the language and cross-cultural management skills required to be effective in many overseas assignments. One crucial difference is that many large American companies have had decades of experience operating in multinational environments, whereas the multinational experience is still quite new for most Japanese organizations. Americans also are native speakers of the international language of management and business—English.

In Japan, the duties of managers who eventually find themselves in North America are multifaceted and complex in ways often unappreciated by North Americans. For instance, employees in a Japanese manager's work group often are not given clearly defined jobs in a North American sense. Instead, as head of the group, a Japanese manager determines priorities and assigns tasks to employees based on his understanding of what needs to be done, rather than by relying on formal job descriptions. Usually, employees will stretch themselves to get those tasks done—even if they don't initially feel prepared and it takes many long workdays to perform to expectations. Japanese managers aren't used to hearing, "I haven't been trained to do that," or "That's not in my job description," or "I'm sorry, but it's quitting time and I'm going home." American managers, on the other hand, are all too familiar with such excuses.

The typical Japanese middle manager's understanding of the differing abilities of employees in his group is based on close, long-term relationships. The manager watches, analyzes, judges, and rewards capable and ambitious employees with important or challenging assignments. While he lets employees know the significance of what they are doing for the company and establishes project deadlines, he frequently leaves the methods of implementation up to them. That, in fact, is one of the primary ways of developing the talents of individuals in the work group—through challenging and pushing them with increasingly important tasks. Formal performance evaluations aren't ignored, but they tend to be perfunctory. Although the manager meets with employees to discuss their work and their careers, coaching and performance feedback tend to be informal and seemingly spontaneous. The manager surrounds employees in an atmosphere of daily advice and admonitions. He seldom sets aside special times to "develop" people.

Japanese observers who have looked at the differences between American and Japanese businesses often cite one major difference that influences all aspects of the way a Japanese organization operates. In Japan, the workplace has almost spiritual dimensions. Like pupils in a temple school, Japanese employees are schooled by discipline, teachings from "masters" (their bosses), and hard work. While Japanese organizations are changing rapidly, this ethos still permeates most major Japanese companies. The regimen is intended to create loyalty and foster the values of the company, and usually it does. Managers feel that one of their responsibilities is creating well-rounded employees with the proper work ethic required by the company. That work ethic includes a willingness to tackle any kind of job earnestly, without questioning the wisdom of the assignment. To Japanese, giving employees wide-ranging assignments will enhance their knowledge and skills; the difficulty of assignments will build an employee's character and cultivate a spirit of perseverance and dedication.

Japanese employees at all levels try to adapt themselves to the direction of the company and learn to move with the atmosphere, climate, or spirit of a meeting or the organization. This ability to sense the shifting *kuuki* (kū-ki) of the organization is intuited from the shifting and unstated assumptions and beliefs operating at the time. Managers who make decisions that are intuitively in sync with the direction of the company are prized. The ideal: an organization that functions like a single entity and reflects the collective will of all employees. Human relationships in such an environment can be complex, and much effort is needed to maintain the harmony that allows such an organization to survive.

Many Japanese companies fall short of the ideal, of course, but it still greatly influences the roles of managers and subordinates. In America and Canada, though, managers and their subordinates tend to see things differently. The workplace tends to be governed by clearly defined contractual obligations, often enforced by law. The fatherly role of many Japanese managers would seem inappropriately paternalistic and strangely out of place in the more impersonal American workplace. "It makes you very uncomfortable," says an American who spent years working for a Japanese company under several Japanese superiors. "I'm a private person, but my bosses often demanded to know my weekend plans or who I was going to see and where I was going to go. To my bosses, this was information they felt they had a right to know. To me, it was none of their business. On those occasions when I explained why this bothered me, I was told, 'It's the Japanese way.' "

Many other things distinguish Japanese managers from North American managers. For example, in Japan, managers might be just as responsible for the performance of work groups as North American managers but, bound by an elaborate and diffuse consensus decision-making process, they might lack the authority to take actions and make decisions that a North American feels are part of acting like a manager. In fact, some observers have argued that Japanese managers are delegated so little authority that they have no choice but to negotiate with subordinates and peers through a consensus process to get anything done at all. Japanese managers admit that making independent decisions is risky—too risky for many, who rely on the consensus process to serve as a kind of safety net; if a decision or change leads to failure, no single individual loses face. When direct action *is* taken by a manager, it must be disguised by the consensus process, which often so effectively diffuses actual authority and power that it seems as if the group decides everything.

FLEXIBILITY FROM INFLEXIBILITY

Why do individuals in Japanese organizations seem to show a flexibility that is so well suited to the challenges of today's fast-changing
global markets? Coral Snodgrass, a North American researcher who
has studied dozens of Japanese companies, argues that individuals
within Japanese organizations typically are more flexible (in the sense
of being tolerant of ambiguous roles and able to work productively
without clear performance objectives and feedback) than workers in
other countries precisely because the Japanese organization itself is so
inflexible.*

That inflexibility can be seen in the strong hierarchies of many
large Japanese companies. New employees advance slowly and methodically through the organization, often maintaining a peer group
solidarity with others in their university graduating class throughout
their careers. Nominal status and rank come more with seniority and
less with achievement or outstanding performance. Relatively early
retirement ages let newer employees move up through the system.
Certainly, individuals of distinction are singled out, but the Japanese
"fast track" is much less obvious than its North American counter-
part.

At the same time, the rules and etiquette of the organization, which
can seem comically elaborate to North Americans, are often rigidly
observed. But there is no contradiction in Japanese organizations
between following the rules and flexibility on the job. The Japanese
hierarchy provides a sense of place. Everyone is assigned a slot in the
hierarchy and trusts the company to act in their own best interests (at
least more than most North Americans would). The strong hierarchical structure makes it unnecessary to continuously redefine relationships. People can adapt to new situations easily, because while
markets and other conditions might change, the form of the organization does not.

* Snodgrass, C., and J. Grant. "Cultural Influences on Strategic Planning and
Control Systems." *Advances in Strategic Management,* Vol. 4, 1986, pp.
205–228.

TSUIKIAI (TSŪ-KĒ-ĂĒ)

Consider as well the importance in Japanese organizations of socializing over drinks with colleagues and subordinates after work is officially over. The image of an inebriated, bone-tired "salaryman" dozing on the commuter train at 11:00 P.M. after spending hours in a Tokyo bar with co-workers is a fixture in the popular North American notion of Japanese business culture. However, Japanese observers say the practice of drinking with colleagues after work is declining, especially among younger Japanese employees, and that typical Japanese office workers go out with colleagues no more than twice a week. Even that seems astonishing to Americans, many of whom focus their off-work time almost exclusively on family and personal activities.

During *tsuikiai* (or socialization), as these semiofficial drinking sessions are sometimes called, much of the real internal business of a Japanese organization is conducted. To many Japanese managers, *tsuikiai* plays an important, sometimes essential, role in communicating performance expectations in their organizations. Drinking parties allow employees to get to know each other outside the formal constraints of the workplace, to be coached and counseled, and to find out what's going on in the rest of the company. Maybe more important, they allow managers to "size up" employees, as one Japanese business consultant puts it, "and determine their ability, motivation, and experiences so tasks can be allocated." Thus, for Japanese managers, in the absence of more formal ways to make such appraisals, *tsuikiai* can provide essential opportunities to fulfill a significant portion of their jobs—informally and intuitively sensing the abilities and potential of subordinates. Of course, American managers often follow their instincts, too, in "sizing up" employees; but as *tsuikiai* and other aspects of the Japanese organization show, the Japanese managers' approach to this hugely important task can be fundamentally different.

THE ENIGMA OF JAPANESE LEADERSHIP

The superior leader gets things done
With very little motion.
He imparts instruction not through many words

But through a few deeds.
He keeps informed about everything
But interferes hardly at all.
He is a catalyst,
And though things wouldn't get done as well
If he wasn't there
When they succeed he takes no credit.
And because he takes no credit
Credit never leaves him.

Be still, manage things quietly,
and keep good control over everything.

As for the leader at the very top,
It is best if people barely know he exists.

LAO-TSU, from *On Leadership*,
sixth century

[Every manager] should spring out of the gate each morning as a
boundary basher. He or she is not just passively "coordinating"
but is aggressively seeking ways to force activity that involves
multiple functions to occur faster. In this new role, the middle
manager must become: (1) expediter/barrier destroyer/
facilitator, (2) on-call expert, and (3) diffuser of good news. In
the short term, [managers] must practice fast-paced "horizontal
management," not traditional, delaying "vertical manage-
ment."

TOM PETERS, from the 1988
U.S. best-seller, *Thriving on*
Chaos

Several experienced observers of Japanese organizations suggest that
Lao-Tsu's prescription for managing and leading still holds true today
in many Japanese organizations. Compared to the frantic, peripatetic
management model described by Tom Peters, a model followed by
many would-be leaders in North American organizations, Japanese
managers and leaders exert influence in far more subtle ways. For
example, they spend more time on informal coaching on the factory
floor and with employee groups. They watch, observe, and carefully
build consensus and collegial relationships. They forge ahead alone
less often than North American managers, and spend far more time

collecting and methodically analyzing data. These differences that characterize Japanese managers can lead to a low-key, unobtrusive— and to North Americans, somewhat "faceless"—management style.

North American managers, especially American managers, rarely spend more than a few minutes on a single task. And unlike Japanese managers, who might focus on getting the organization to run by itself, American managers often feel more compelled to try to do everything themselves. North American managers also are far more likely to be involved in outside professional activities and, in the case of senior executives, are more likely to sit on the boards of directors of other companies, which further fragments their time. Japanese managers, by contrast, are more likely to be totally immersed in their companies, to which they probably have committed their entire careers. They have an extremely wide knowledge of their organizations (because they have been rotated through so many parts of the organization), and they rely on internal, informal contacts and the collective energy of the group.

In addition to dealing with a management style that is unfamiliar to North Americans, Japanese managers face another challenge. Overseas assignments in any multinational organization, especially Japanese organizations, can be temporary and sometimes quite short. The Japanese practice of moving people around from operation to operation is one way Japanese companies develop and maintain organizational flexibility. But, according to many Americans working for Japanese organizations, the frequent rotation of senior managers makes management continuity difficult and often hampers the development of Japanese managers as effective leaders in North America. This is especially true when Japanese presidents are reassigned every two or three years. "Every executive sent over here is a lame-duck president to begin with," complains one American manager. "After two or three years, they're sent back home. This revolving door of executives means you have difficulty getting a feeling for where the company is going or, for that matter, who even runs the company."

This American's complaint might surprise Japanese workers, who seem to find changes in leadership less disruptive. They know, as one Japanese executive puts it, that an "invisible system" is running the organization and that, while personalities might change, "little else does." But Americans, used to more individualistic rather than collective management, have learned that changes at the top can mean tremendous operational changes as well. "When we got our latest [Japanese] president," this American continues, "I told him I've had too many bosses in the last six years, and every time you change, we're dead in the water for six months." He adds:

> You finally get to know someone and understand how he thinks, and then he's gone. Nothing really happens when a new boss arrives. Everyone is waiting to find out what his agenda is. His hot buttons might be different from his predecessor's, and no one is going to do anything until they figure out what his hot buttons are.

Because new Japanese managers might come from different areas of the organization, new general managers or presidents often seem to have little in common with their predecessors. Their management styles, whims, and preferences can be completely different.

Thus, one challenge facing Japanese organizations in America is how to help American employees transfer their allegiance from strong leaders (and the loyalty to one's turf, department, unit, or clique that is created) to the organization. Sometimes it works. At Mitsubishi's U.S. sales subsidiary, a senior American vice-president says the traditional "caste system" that characterizes U.S. automakers is absent. "Our people don't think about which executive they work for, just what projects they are working on."* Other Japanese organizations have been successful at making the transition as well, but the need of many Americans for a strong, continuous management presence continues to run counter to Japanese practices.

FEAR OF LETTING GO

"We don't have the authority to *do,* although we have the authority to deny," notes a Japanese manager with sadness. The remark reflects a dilemma many North Americans in Japanese companies perceive as being at the heart of the Japanese leadership challenge in North America: Japanese managers in North America are unable to "let go" by involving local managers in decision making and operational policy because they themselves have so little room to maneuver.

* *Business Month,* April 1990, p. 60.

Fear might have something to do with it, too. For Japanese companies with big plans and massive investments in North America, the stakes have become very high. A North American assignment, once akin to exile, is now considered an honor and a sign that a manager might be on his way to the top. The risks of letting North American managers have an active role in operations have to be weighed carefully against the odds that they might not do as good a job as a Japanese manager. Consequently, giving up some degree of control is seen as a slow, evolutionary process. Frequently, however, the process grinds to a halt without ever really beginning. Ultimately, this lack of progress leads to the feeling among North American managers that they aren't trusted or even respected by their Japanese colleagues.

It has been noted by numerous observers that failure is the greatest fear of Japanese managers in North America. While that fear might seem universal, it can be argued that Japanese managers labor under a heavier psychological burden. Individual success for Japanese managers might not bring the same rewards that it brings to North American managers—but individual failure can be far more punishing. With their greater job mobility, North American managers have an easier time leaving their failures behind them. Even the most successful North American manager probably has a resume that includes jobs that "didn't quite work out."

On the other hand, Japanese managers, who expect to work for the same employer all their lives, have a more difficult time ducking the consequences of their actions. Failure to a North American manager might mean a temporary slip on the ascent up the corporate ladder; failure to a Japanese manager might mean falling off the ladder completely.

When they assess their dissatisfaction with life in a Japanese company, North Americans often say their perceived fear of failure, as well as the suffocating daily control exercised by headquarters, are among the underlying obstacles to their greater involvement in decision and policy making. "Any manager is worried that when you delegate authority, things are going to blow up in your face," says an American manager. But in North America, that fear is almost paralyzing for the Japanese. According to this same American:

> Japanese managers have a sense that they can't control Americans, that Americans aren't motivated by the right things. They've told me this.

They feel that if you give Americans responsibility for something, they think they've got a blank check to go off and do it their own way. Japanese managers are great at delegating tasks among themselves—they don't impose strict controls and guidelines, and they make the person charged with the task sweat out the details. When that person needs help, he knows how to go to his managers and solicit their advice without making it seem like he's asking them what to do.

But they pull back with Americans because they think Americans are always so concerned about proving themselves. Their experiences with Americans tell them that Americans don't want help or to be checked up on. They resent it as interference. Their job becomes part of their territory, so to speak, and Japanese managers don't like people to think they have their own territory. They're afraid Americans are going to get possessive and act independently. Too much of either of those things is not good in a Japanese company.

Others note that the "relational" management style of Japanese companies, typified by consensus decision making, long-term personal ties, and exquisite attention paid to internal politics in Japanese organizations, can lead to paralysis in overseas operations. When Japanese companies discover that "overseas acquisitions and joint ventures can't be managed long distance from Tokyo in the familiar 'consensus' style," says Yoshimichi Yamashita, head of the Japanese branch of a U.S. consulting firm, "Japanese managers overseas are unable or unwilling to act on their own. What results is inertia."

CONFUSION OVER THE PRIVILEGES OF RANK

One of the first things many North Americans notice about the Japanese is the bowing and other signs of deference shown to higher status or ranking individuals. Some have seen Japanese executives prostrate themselves on the floor in a symbol of extreme deference to visiting executives. "When the big boss comes from Japan, he gets a royal treatment like we never gave a Canadian boss," says a manager from Toronto. "One Japanese executive found out what hotel his boss was staying at and waited in the lobby for nine hours just so he could help him check in."

The importance of observing status and rank is confusing to North American managers because it conflicts with many of the very appealing egalitarian aspects of Japanese organizations—executives and employees eating together, wearing the same uniforms, and so forth. It also goes against fundamental American attitudes since it seems to imply that some people are better than others. As a plant manager from Georgia put it, "Just because I am this man's boss doesn't make me any better than him. It just means at the end of the day my vote is worth 51 percent and his is worth 49 percent." The plant manager goes on to say:

> Some Japanese managers seem to think Americans have a
> lack of respect for managers because they do not do a lot
> of what Americans consider "bowing and scraping." But
> it has nothing to do with that. Americans just don't see the
> significance of it, and even if they did, they wouldn't do it
> anyway.

Japanese managers bow and otherwise honor individuals of higher status and rank because they have been brought up to do so as a sign of respect, and, frankly, some do it to make a good impression on their bosses—just as American managers do. It is just a different way of trying to ingratiate themselves than would be found in North America. In Japan, as in North America, true respect is appreciated, and exaggerated displays are frowned on and even laughed at. To the Japanese, exaggerated or out-of-proportion gestures are seen as "toad eating," among other contemptuous terms.

3

THROUGH JAPANESE EYES:

THE SELF-CENTERED NORTH AMERICAN MANAGER

I have given up trying to teach them about our culture and business practices. They don't want to learn.

JAPANESE MANAGER

We can learn much from how they balance work and life, and how they sell their ideas.

JAPANESE MANAGER

WHAT'S IT LIKE TO WORK WITH NORTH AMERICANS?

WHAT ARE AMERICAN managers like to work with? What strengths and weaknesses do they bring to Japanese-American workplaces? Some insight into these questions comes from an unpublished study of the perceptions held by Japanese employees working for U.S.-owned financial concerns in Japan.

The most common observation of Japanese co-workers: North Americans rarely make much effort to learn and understand Japanese culture and customs. Many have been here for years, the Japanese often complained, yet they're just as American as ever. And these same foreigners are often the ones who complain that the Japanese marketplace and Japanese society are "closed" to outsiders.

The reasons for attempting to learn Japanese customs—and especially simple, everyday expressions—are obvious: If the company is Japanese, foreign employees who don't learn Japanese can never expect to advance beyond a certain level. And if the company is a joint venture or a foreign operation attempting to thrive in the Japanese market, the same ignorance will make an adequate understanding of Japanese business customs and management philosophies impossible.

But the real complaint of many Japanese is the inability of North Americans to adjust to the Japanese way of running an organization, an approach many Japanese respondents admitted probably involves a number of uniquely Japanese, "nonrational" characteristics. For instance, even after years in Japan, North Americans remain so confounded by basic aspects of Japanese organizations such as consensus decision making and preliminary negotiation methods (*nemawashi* [nā-mă-wă-she]) that "patient and endless explanation is required," as one Japanese respondent said, before Japanese and North Americans can accomplish even minor tasks together.

One reason for this dilemma, Japanese co-workers feel, is the fact that North Americans place so little emphasis on communication within departments and among individuals that it is difficult for them to work in groups. "They go off and do what they want to do," said one Japanese, "with no appreciation for the effects of what they do on others." With their "emphasis on promoting individual ability and achievement, the good part of group dynamics among Americans is pushed aside," said another Japanese. "Moreover," said a third, "because of their excessive self-assertiveness, it is hard for them to listen to opinions that are different from their own." This focus on the self also corresponds with an excessive emphasis on specialization, which makes it difficult for North Americans to be well rounded.

The Japanese also noticed that North Americans don't seem to understand the dualism of many of their Japanese colleagues—the outward calm expression that preserves group harmony and the sometimes quite emotional inward nature. "Because they are all surface," said one Japanese of North Americans, "they fail to appreciate the distinction between outward behavior and inner feelings, which

causes endless minor and major communication problems." The tendency of North Americans "to act and talk aggressively" also makes
it difficult for them to appreciate subtlety and nuance in business
relationships. They don't grasp the difference, for instance, between
phrases like "general meaning" and "precise meaning." They are
very opinionated, holding to their opinions no matter what the evidence suggests. There is only one way to look at things—namely,
their way—and this leads to superficial analysis and poor decisions.

The individual and business priorities of North Americans also
seem misplaced to Japanese co-workers. North American decision
makers focus on pleasing stockholders and their bosses back home
and on individual, self-centered personal gain, rather than on long-
term, market-share-building strategies and measures. This leads them
to make shortsighted judgments based on what appears to be right or
wrong under immediate circumstances, not on future implications or
the wholeness of a plan or policy. North American executives also
seem surprisingly indifferent to the welfare of employees. They take
the very un-Japanese view that employees are just another business
expense and are quick to consider trimming payrolls to maintain profit
levels.

On a daily basis, Japanese employees found that their North American co-workers frequently place an inappropriate emphasis on their
private lives. They seem obsessed with vacations, time off, and plans
for family activities. This creates friction, Japanese respondents said,
not only because it seems to indicate a lack of job commitment but
also because the attitude is a luxury few Japanese think they can
afford. "By no means is it necessarily good to work all the time,"
sighed one Japanese, "but the Japanese work diligently without any
choice. When foreign nationals take long vacations, or *any* vacation, it
creates a thick wall in business life."

This focus on private lives is also seen in the reluctance of North
Americans to participate in what one Japanese calls "Japanese-style
friendship activities." He is referring to *tsuikiai,* the practice of
meeting in bars and restaurants after-hours to carry on a combination
of business and social activities. North Americans seem to divide the
day more sharply than their Japanese colleagues. To North Americans, when work is over, another phase of one's life begins—the
personal and private. To the Japanese (males in particular), work and
identity, business and pleasure, are closely intertwined.

The same is true when it comes to business partners in other companies. Many Japanese business relationships and "deals" are cemented informally outside the office. North Americans lack the ability to cultivate these relationships and are relatively insensitive to the many nuances that govern them. The reason is their failure to appreciate the importance of after-hours business socialization, which limits their effectiveness as businesspeople in Japan. "To succeed in Japan, North Americans need to associate more with Japanese outside the office," one Japanese complains, "but they don't understand that business continues outside of work."

"Outside of work" to North Americans includes the personal sphere, which often involves family members. Japanese co-workers find this involvement of families to be confusing and somewhat distasteful. North Americans sometimes want to bring spouses and children to "social" events, complain Japanese co-workers, without understanding that these events are really quasibusiness functions where family members are inappropriate. Bringing wives to "business" dinners is especially confusing to Japanese males. "What are you supposed to say to someone's wife?" one Japanese male asked. "Why do they insist on bringing them?"

RIGID MENTALITIES

One of the greatest barriers encountered by the Japanese was the obstinate conviction of North Americans that their way of viewing a situation was absolutely correct, and their rigid insistence on certain simplistic notions regarding workplace equality and fairness. North Americans seem unable to consider different or opposing viewpoints or to arrive at a synthesis based on the input of many. Because of this "mental inflexibility," said one Japanese respondent, "Americans spend far too much time learning from their mistakes—and then they don't end up learning that much."

According to the Japanese, this lack of flexibility is apparent in the fact that North Americans are so tied to specific bosses that they become somewhat bewildered and disoriented when those bosses are replaced. "It requires painstaking effort to help them adjust when senior managers and bosses are replaced," one Japanese respondent said. Policy changes have a similar effect on North Americans. This helplessness was explained, in part, by rigid North American notions about how organizations are supposed to function. Lines of communication, chains of command, and reporting relationships assume an importance greatly out of proportion to the actual running of the business. "Without these things, they don't know what to do," marveled one Japanese, who wondered how Americans had ever achieved a reputation for initiative and independence.

Many Japanese respondents in the survey believed the major source of tension between North Americans and Japanese in the workplace was caused by the North Americans seeing things too logically and rationally. There is much in Japanese business, the respondents acknowledged, that North Americans find *nonrational,* which is not the same to the Japanese as irrational. Look at how North Americans respond to claims, overdue payments, and contractual obligations, Japanese respondents said. They're all so practical and efficient. If a contract says an obligation must be met by a certain date, that's that— a contract is a contract, and terms are terms. But business relations are vastly more complex, the Japanese say. The North American insistence on legalities prevents them from understanding how to "stand alongside the customer." It prevents them from understanding how to "represent the company as a whole." They think that everything should be put on paper and "somehow that settles it."

MUCH TO ADMIRE

It should be noted that many Japanese respondents mixed their reservations about their North American colleagues with admiration and envy. For example, being opinionated and self-centered also means that many North Americans appear relatively fearless about expressing their thoughts and ideas, even to their superiors. "And their bosses think this is normal," said one admiring Japanese co-worker. When clarity and decisiveness are needed, this trait is one many Japanese respondents thought they would do well to emulate.

The Japanese also remarked on their foreign colleagues' ability to express and argue for opposing positions during meetings and conferences "and not carry ill feelings over into other activities and personal affairs," as one Japanese put it. He added that for many Japanese, honest disagreement needlessly poisons relationships.

The differences in prioritizing, which so many Japanese seem to resent, can also produce grudging admiration. "They enjoy their work with a free spirit," one Japanese said. "They work to enjoy life, since their first priority is on their private lives." On the job, many Japanese perceive North Americans as being better at managing their time and at "classifying and dealing with tasks according to their importance." To these Japanese, the not-strictly-rational Japanese style makes powerful and enduring organizations possible, but it doesn't always represent the most efficient or most personally satisfying way of getting things done.

4

LIVING IN NORTH AMERICA

---

*We had such grand plans. We knew it would be important to get
to know each other as friends and neighbors as we planned and
built the facility. We rented condominiums in the same place. We
figured we'd hang around the pool, go out to dinner, do things
after work. We discovered, however, that when the workday
ended, the Americans went one way, the Japanese the other way.
There just didn't seem to be anything we could do about it.*

AMERICAN MANAGER
DISCUSSING A JOINT JAPANESE-
U.S. VENTURE

THE BEST INTENTIONS

A HEAVY EQUIPMENT manufacturer in the Midwest discovered the hard
way what many Japanese operations in North America eventually
discover: Throwing North Americans and Japanese together in the
workplace does not automatically produce the bonds of trust and
friendship that mark a cohesive and effective management team. One
American manager says he and the other Americans were troubled
until they realized that, "After spending the whole day struggling to
speak English and understand our ways, the last thing the Japanese

wanted to do was hang around with us after work. They needed a chance to get away from the pressure, and socializing with us just represented more pressure."

Few Japanese organizations expect new operations to succeed without some type of active process to familiarize North American and Japanese employees with one another's cultures. Usually, North American and Japanese managers work together from the inception of any Japanese operation in North America on programs to promote cultural understanding and friendships inside and outside the workplace. Unfortunately, evidence suggests that such efforts are often halfhearted and inconsistent, and they frequently fail to recognize the actual immensity of the challenge. Programs to socialize and "acculturate" Japanese and North Americans are often based on naive assumptions—the suburban idyll described at the beginning of this chapter illustrates how easily North Americans believe cultural integration can be achieved.

If Japanese managers are fortunate, their companies provide a period of intense cultural immersion before their North American assignment begins. For instance, NEC's Institute for International Studies near Tokyo serves as a kind of "boot camp" for NEC managers about to begin international assignments. Its 162 courses cover everything from cocktail-party small talk to North American labor law. As in similar programs run by other Japanese companies, translating the highly nuanced Japanese way of communicating into an English that can be understood by North Americans requires great effort. NEC instructors report that they spend much of their time trying to get Japanese managers to learn simply to say, "I disagree," "I agree," or "I have no idea."

Similarly, if North American managers new to a Japanese company are lucky, part of their orientation will include a visit to the parent organization in Japan. These visits have several important benefits. They give North American managers a clear picture of how the company operates and they see how the company's values, which can sound rather vague in North America, are translated into actual day-to-day operations. Visits to Japan also turn the tables and put North Americans at a language disadvantage. This helps increase their sensitivity to the magnitude of the communication challenge Japanese managers face in North America. Just as important, it demystifies Japan and Japanese life; discerning North Americans quickly realize that despite the many obvious differences, Japanese and North Americans have much in common.

Unfortunately, most Japanese and American managers receive more superficial orientations. A one-week course or orientation visit is all that most managers can hope for. As a result, they come to their new environments very unprepared.

A CONFUSINGLY CASUAL CULTURE

No amount of advanced preparation can completely immunize Japanese managers to the disorienting effects of North American culture and society. In fact, some of the most disorienting aspects of life in North America are among the most basic to its society. As we've seen from the reactions of Japanese who work with North Americans in Japan, different approaches to family life can surprise and even shock Japanese managers when they come to North America. For instance, company-sponsored "open houses," picnics, and other social events involving spouses and children are common in North America. Japanese managers frequently find such events strange and uncomfortable. Many North American managers report that their Japanese colleagues almost have to be forced to bring their families to family-oriented company events. "They are definitely not happy about the idea," says one American manager. "We go round and round endlessly about it. It makes the annual picnic pretty grim."

Another manager recalls the organization's Christmas party:

We have an annual Christmas dinner, followed by dancing. Attendance is considered to be compulsory unless the staff member is on vacation or sick. Even the arranging of vacations around this time is frowned upon. The Japanese staff hate this annual event. They turn up with their wives, usually sit in groups, rarely mixing, and normally leave the moment the meal is over!

Not all Japanese managers are surprised by such events, however. It depends on the culture of the home operation. One Japanese manager in the United States who spent several years with IBM Japan in Tokyo notes that while IBM Japan was staffed predominantly by Japanese, family affairs were held regularly, and most Japanese employees thoroughly enjoyed such events. Many Americans who have worked in Japan also have attended work-related affairs to which family members were invited. But the traditional Japanese view that public (business) and private (family) matters should never be mixed is still very strong. Efforts to break down the barrier between the two are sometimes resisted by Japanese managers in America.

One American manager recalls a Sunday afternoon drive that he and his family took with a new Japanese colleague and his family. The trip took them past the plant, a U.S.-Japanese joint venture, which was virtually deserted for the day. To the American manager, it was a perfect opportunity to stop and show the children the plant. "Every kid has seen where his or her dad works," the American observes. "But my Japanese friend was visibly upset by the suggestion. I dropped the idea after we stopped in the parking lot, and it became clear that he intended to order his family to stay in the car."

Informal social occasions, in which employees from different levels mix, seem especially uncomfortable for Japanese managers. Many North American managers say they've invited a Japanese co-worker and his spouse over to the house for a few drinks or a backyard barbecue, only to have the invitation declined because the boss was not invited. Many Japanese employees seem unwilling to risk the potential offense to their superiors. "We gave up on the 'come on over Friday, bring the wife and kids, and we'll put a few steaks on the fire' thing," says one U.S. manager, "because we couldn't socialize together unless it was formal, with everyone's rank and status observed."

"It's high-tension time," another American manager says of such events. "Regrettably," the manager adds, "since such events are intended to reduce social tensions, not heighten them. They're especially hard for the [Japanese] wives, who might not speak English well and are not used to meeting their husbands' co-workers and superiors in a social setting. They seem very self-conscious about not dressing the right way or saying the right thing, and their husbands don't seem to let up on them. It's painful to see how they are unable to relax in such settings."

One reason for the relative unease of some Japanese colleagues in social situations, often overlooked by Americans, is the fact that living arrangements in Japan encourage different ways of entertaining than are typically found in North America. For example, private homes in Japan are often too small to accommodate groups of guests beyond close family members, whereas in the sprawling suburbs of North America, homes are designed with entertaining in mind. And, as noted, entertaining in Japan is often done within the confines of male-only work groups in bars and restaurants close to the office. It's a small wonder, then, that casual American-style social events, with the American husband or wife entertaining guests as equals, often with children present, can create a barrage of culturally confusing signals. Meanwhile, the workplace itself can be especially barren for Japanese employees in North America, because in Japan it serves as the focal point for social relationships, whereas in America, employees are likely to head home as soon as the official workday is over.

Some hint of the tension produced by attempts to socialize with North Americans comes from the Japanese Health and Welfare Ministry, which reported that a 1990 survey of nearly 1,000 Japanese managers and their families in overseas posts showed that a substantial number suffered what the Ministry called "slight nervous breakdowns," due primarily to language and culture problems. Wives, only 20 percent of whom could communicate in the language of the country in which they were posted, seemed to suffer the most. While Middle Eastern cultures were the most troublesome, nearly one out of five Japanese wives in the United States and Canada reported some kind of pronounced mental distress.*

FAMILY NEEDS AND OBLIGATIONS

The differences between Japanese and North Americans are sometimes most obvious when family matters arise. In fact, North Americans in Japanese organizations will often say that Japanese attitudes toward family matters loom as one of the biggest sources of conflict. "Japanese managers must understand that many, if not most, North Americans will not even question choosing a family need over a work requirement," says a Canadian manager. The issue arises in many forms in Japanese-North American workplaces. Sometimes, the family need or obligation is such that no one can reasonably equate it with

* "Mental Distress Cited by Wives Living with Men Sent Abroad." *Japan Times*, July 25, 1990, p. 2.

questionable employee loyalty or commitment to the company—attending the birth of a child instead of staying late to finish a project, for example, or medical emergencies that involve immediate family members. Yet many North Americans conclude that it's difficult for Japanese managers to feel much empathy for the life they lead outside the workplace—or for the fact that families in North America are often headed by single parents whose challenges are often far more time-consuming than the typical two-parent Japanese family, consisting of the male breadwinner and a full-time housewife and mother.

Just-in-time production, the lean staffing of Japanese operations, and other factors make it especially difficult for many single parents in the North American work force to balance the personal and business aspects of life. Japanese organizations can't discriminate against hiring single parents in North America; yet, according to many North Americans employed by them, far too few of these organizations seem to understand how to accommodate the needs of single parents. "They cut you no slack," says an American production worker, a single father of two, who adds that he's lost track of the number of times overtime was announced an hour or two before his shift was supposed to end. The strain this puts on his parental obligations is immense, the worker says.

"In Japan, wives handle everything," another American production employee asserts in a widely shared view. "There's no need for Japanese males to respond to anything but work. There's no day-to-day involvement in family affairs. But when you're the sole breadwinner and sole parent, when you've got to find day care and doctors and worry about what's happening at school, trying to tune out family needs for ten hours a day is impossible."

What seems to contribute to the perception that Japanese managers "aren't particularly interested in what's happening in your life," as an American woman puts it, is the fact that Japanese managers often don't have the luxury of working less than twelve-, fourteen-, or even sixteen-hour days—sometimes six days a week. "They just martyr themselves," says an American manager. "When you work so hard, it's easy to resent those who don't." If Japanese managers feel isolated from their surrounding communities, or are housed in company dormitories, as are many Japanese trainers and production advisors on short-term assignments, the workplace can become the sum total of their existence. "Our ideas of what's important and where priorities lie are completely reversed," says an American woman who has worked for a Japanese financial services company in California for several years. "Most Americans I know seem to be working longer hours than ever, but at the same time we've become aware of trying to balance work with family and leisure time. The Japanese make great sacrifices in these areas, and it's hard for them to understand where we're coming from."

Similarly, North Americans might believe that something as funda- mental as sick time or vacation also can cast a shadow on their perceived commitment to a Japanese company. One Japanese com- pany put its feelings about sick time in writing and was truly embar- rassed when the memo was reproduced in the humor column of the *London Financial Times* under the title, "Feeling Better?":

"FEELING BETTER?"

All staff are requested to ensure that their bodies are maintained in such a way that is conducive to a healthier, wealthier, and happier being. Please remember that excessive sick leave will be reflected in Septem- ber bonuses and subsequent annual salary reviews.

> Nikko Capital Management (UK),
> in a memorandum to staff,
> *London Financial Times,*
> June 19, 1992

Stories about the efforts of Japanese government agencies and business groups to encourage Japanese workers to take time off have been widely reported by the North American media. The stories are greeted with amusement because North American usually need few inducements to take their annual vacations. North Americans in Japa- nese companies may get the sense, however, that Japanese managers in North America believe that taking vacations when production needs are tight represents a kind of desertion. Most North Americans realize that this sentiment is due not so much to insensitivity as it is to the tremendous pressures on Japanese managers to bring operations up to Japanese levels of productivity.

To some extent, the demands of Japanese organizations are legiti- mate and are clearly linked to the system that creates their famous quality and productivity. The typical Japanese production system cannot tolerate the same degree of absenteeism found in many North American companies. Persuading employees to accept this change often requires a fundamental change of values. Still, the pressures Japanese managers face often add to the sense of perpetual crisis some North Americans report experiencing in Japanese workplaces. "We are a multibillion-dollar company with a fairly secure future," says an American manager who has worked for the same Japanese company for nearly a decade. "Yet everything continues to be presented as this life-or-death struggle. You just can't let up for a minute. The expectation of continual sacrifice really takes a toll—on the Japanese and on us."

FORCING IT?

Japanese and North American human resources experts, line and staff managers, and others often use the word *purposeful* in describing the way socialization should work in the Japanese-North American workplace. "The people who play together do better in their work relationships," says one American human resources director. "But mixing has to be pursued vigilantly."

The most common way North American and Japanese co-workers try to get to know one another is through quasibusiness drinking after work, but *tsuikiai* may be an imperfect mechanism for the purposeful socialization process many people believe Japanese and North Americans need. For several reasons, work-related drinking might never serve the same function in North America—at least among North Americans—that it serves in Japan. Because speaking English after work offers no respite to Japanese managers after the exhausting challenge of communicating in English during a long workday, after-work conversation in bars and restaurants often breaks into two groups—American and Japanese. "Social drinking after work makes you feel more separate than ever," says an American in California. Also, many North American managers prefer to spend at least a part of each day with their spouses and children. For that reason alone, routinely spending an hour or two in a bar after an already long workday is simply not an option for many North Americans.

North Americans are also drinking less, as evidenced by the fact that alcoholic consumption in the United States and Canada has been declining steadily for most of the past decade. Law enforcement agencies, employers, insurance companies, and society at large have been pushing the trend. Today, North American health clubs often are more crowded after work than bars and restaurants. And while this is hardly scientific, many North American managers say they neither desire nor are able to consume as much liquor as Japanese colleagues. "The Japanese just flat out drink more than we do," says an American manager, who for that reason dreads his occasional visits to the home office in Tokyo, which he says take on the characteristics of an exhausting drinking marathon. "Even if you wanted to, you couldn't keep up with their pace."

SO, WHAT WORKS?

Elements of a purposeful socialization process, tried with varying degrees of success at Japanese organizations in North America, include:

• **Intense programs to introduce Japanese managers to the customs and culture of North America.** Most Japanese managers receive some brief cultural training in Japan. But the ineffectiveness of such training can be judged by the vast cultural differences that immediately become apparent between Japanese and North American colleagues, and the often surprising naiveté (at least to North Americans) of many senior Japanese personnel regarding cultural, legal, and human resources issues in North America. Given their manpower needs in North America, many Japanese companies have no choice but to send managers whose experience and training leave them inadequately prepared for the dramatically different North American scene. Whenever possible, Japanese companies should invest in more comprehensive training for their North America-bound managers (see Chapter 17).

One area in which training can help is in understanding North American attitudes toward *tsuikiai*. Japanese managers can interpret an unwillingness to participate in after-hours drinking as job dissatisfaction or lack of interest and dedication. Cultural orientation can help put things in the correct light.

• **Commitments to full and truthful communications.** As noted, commitments among North Americans and Japanese to speak one language (always English), never meet separately, and never segregate themselves during coffee breaks and other slack periods frequently fall by the wayside as communication problems escalate or tensions increase. Such a total commitment to English is difficult for Japanese managers, and can be humiliating for those who speak English especially poorly. Many Japanese organizations, however, realize that some mechanism has to be in place to encourage the use of English. The problem is developing one that doesn't make impossible demands on Japanese managers. One Japanese organization forces Japanese managers to make a sizable contribution to a local charity if they are caught speaking Japanese when Americans are in the room. The method may be extreme, but the goal is important—clear and complete communications, with nothing hidden, that eliminates the potential for confusion and mistrust. The same goal can be reached in many creative ways, as long as both sides keep trying. In general, North Americans don't mind Japanese managers talking in their native tongue. However, they do mind when they feel their Japanese colleagues are using their language to be less than forthright in sharing ideas and information.

• **Structured social events as part of assimilation programs between coordinators/advisors and their North American counterparts/trainees.** Realistically, it might be too great a cultural jump for Japanese managers to go from socializing among themselves in work groups to the more family-oriented North American style of socializing. An easier transition might be made by socializing with North Americans within work groups through bowling and other sporting activities. Toyota, among other Japanese companies in North America, covers some of the costs of mixed socializing.

• **Development of social skills.** Many Japanese managers who have developed good working relationships with North Americans and an understanding of North American society say they try to become knowledgeable about one facet of North American life (mainly sports, politics, popular entertainment, or local community issues) as a kind of hobby and as a means of developing something in common with their North American colleagues. Baseball and football are, of course, the great American pastimes. "If you can talk about football, you can carry on a conversation with almost anyone," says one Japanese manager who has read several books about North American football and diligently follows the scores in American newspapers. This is very natural for Japanese because, compared to their American counterparts, Japanese tend to focus on one activity or sport and stay with it for many years until they become highly adept at it.

• **A formal mentoring system for Japanese managers and their families.** New employees and their families can be paired with a more experienced Japanese employee and his family, who act as guides, confidants, and sources of moral support in the strange new North American cultural environment. Many Japanese companies already have such mentors—individuals whose language skills and cultural sensitivity are developed enough to buffer some of the cultural and personal problems that arise in the mixed Japanese-North American workplace. A Japanese human resources coordinator often serves this purpose—although the position is purely informal and such individuals are often hard pressed to keep up with the demand.

More efforts, formal or informal, are needed to bridge cultural gaps. Evidence suggests these gaps are not narrowed merely by time. Programs to initially prepare Japanese managers for North American assignments can be ineffective because, as many Japanese managers admit, so much information is thrown at them that little is actually retained. A better approach might involve an initial orientation, then ongoing education over the first two years of a Japanese manager's North American assignment. Of course, this might be easier to contemplate than to implement, given the work intensity of many Japanese organizations.

ROLE OF NORTH AMERICANS

For smooth socialization to be realistic at all, North Americans must share the responsibility with their Japanese colleagues. One consideration is the timing of social events. With their strong work ethic and their habit of working late, Japanese managers often are ill at ease with activities that start right after work. Often, they just won't take part. Saturday activities are much more acceptable.

We've noted the difficulty North Americans encounter in attempting to learn the Japanese language. This doesn't mean North Americans can't work harder at better understanding the business and nonbusiness aspects of Japanese culture. New Japanese operations in North America frequently will host activities designed to promote cultural familiarization. The efforts, however, often seem short-lived and fairly ineffective. For example, the wives of Japanese managers might demonstrate traditional Japanese crafts and skills, such as flower arranging and tea ceremonies. However, while such activities might hint at the depth and complexity of Japanese tradition and history, they often provide little insight into modern Japanese life.

An alternate approach that seems to stimulate North Americans to learn more about Japanese life uses commercial videotapes on Japanese culture and society. When followed by a discussion, the videos provide Japanese colleagues and their wives with excellent opportunities to introduce North Americans to the realities of contemporary Japanese life and society. While Japanese viewers might question the way some of these productions depict their lives, these videos have proved useful for stimulating discussions with North Americans about the many differences—and similarities—that exist between the two cultures. At the very least, they provide a tool to help erase popular North American misconceptions of modern Japanese life, and the sometimes damaging effects those misconceptions can produce in the workplace. The best video series we have seen is *Nippon: The Land and Its People,* developed by Nippon Steel Human Resources Development Co., Ltd., based on the book by the same title.

Of course, one of the best ways of bridging the cultural gap is for North Americans to visit Japan. Even a superficial "tourist" visit has benefits, but a more orchestrated, cultural orientation can pay even greater dividends.

STRESS FACTORS: COMMON PROBLEMS FOR JAPANESE MANAGERS IN NORTH AMERICA

Career Anxiety: A North American assignment can produce feelings of isolation from the mainstream of the Japanese organization. No matter how important the assignment, Japanese managers might fear that the distance and isolation from headquarters will delay or even damage advancement. Meanwhile, the isolation and limited feedback can add to the pressure to perform.

Managing North Americans: Many Japanese managers might find themselves with subordinates for the first time—and Americans at that. Trying to understand the Americans' more egocentric motivations, relative unfamiliarity with working in teams, and tendency to view team contributions as less important than individual contributions, as well as their personal demands and many more differences, makes the challenge immense.

Fitting In: With limited English-language skills and different cultural habits and expectations, developing friendships beyond a circle of other Japanese employees can be very difficult, because socializing informally with Americans and their families is so different. The workplace, which is not the focus of social life in America, does not provide the natural and personal communications to which the Japanese are accustomed.

Academic Pressures: Many Japanese parents in America worry that their children might not receive an education that meets Japanese standards—especially when it comes to being prepared for college entrance exams. Special remedial schools on weekends are common. Japanese parents also worry that their children might become over-assimilated, or seduced, by American culture.

PART TWO

—————

JAPANESE AND NORTH AMERICANS IN THE WORKPLACE

5

"WALK LIKE YOU TALK":

THE CHALLENGE OF COMMUNICATING VISION AND VALUES IN THE JAPANESE ORGANIZATION

The Japanese here work with such a life-or-death intensity. They've got this strong survival ethic, despite the fact that they seem to have survived very well. To them, you've got to sacrifice, push, struggle without reward. When I tell them that in order for us to push kaizen, *we've got to celebrate people's efforts and come up with a communication plan to show them what all of this means, they say, "No, no, no. We have to make people aware our survival is at stake." But presenting it in those terms doesn't work here. People are less concerned with survival of this enterprise than with what they get for their effort.*

AMERICAN MANAGER

The Japanese need to learn to walk like they talk.

AMERICAN MANAGER

CULTURE/COUNTERCULTURE

Two Japanese companies operate similar manufacturing operations in the same American city. The plants are only a few miles from each other. Each employs about the same number of local workers. Each has the same functional, no-frills exterior. But inside, the two plants are very different.

In one, if you ask local production employees how they like their jobs, they'll acknowledge that their jobs are demanding, overtime is frequently required, and there is little room for "goofing off" or taking it easy. Yet they also say that somehow these jobs are very satisfying. Each day presents unique and exciting challenges. Quality, continuous improvement—it all makes sense. The Japanese coordinators, production engineers, and advisors who work alongside them have done a good job of explaining the rationale behind the production process, which manages to be simple and sophisticated at the same time. It's easy to think in their terms. Uniforms, for instance, are voluntary, but virtually all the Americans wear them. Arriving a few minutes before one's shift begins would be crazy at an American operation, but here *kaizen* (kī-zĕn), continuous improvement, far from being some mystical concept, is practiced daily in many small ways. The company isn't out to change the world, but many of the things the Japanese do themselves and expect of the Americans seem to work for the benefit of everyone.

The American managers tell a similar story—the hours are long, the pace is demanding, but it's a good place to work. Many of them are sent regularly to Japan, where it's easy to see just what the company means about participation, teamwork, and other values— values that might otherwise degenerate into empty and, to American ears, somewhat silly-sounding slogans.

At the second Japanese operation, employees have heard some of the same words—participation, teamwork, continuous productivity improvement, and so on—but the effects have been very different. Here, employees feel they have little to show for their efforts. The policies of their Japanese employer are inconsistent and confusing, despite the frequent exhortations to work hard and make "great contributions" to the glory of the company and its noble enterprise. Japanese managers and coordinators are not easy to get along with.

Sometimes their actions make little sense. Explanations of why things are done a certain way are rarely forthcoming. They push you very hard here, employees say. But what, they ask, are *we* getting out of it?

This question is never answered to anyone's satisfaction. One consequence is that employees rarely are willing to make an extra effort, to the great consternation of the Japanese. Employees, in fact, ignore much of what the Japanese say or, if possible, do just the opposite. They get more satisfaction from petty acts of insubordination than from doing a "good job" as defined by the Japanese. The American managers aren't much help to the Japanese. They seem just as restless and dissatisfied as the production employees. The company's relentless focus on pursuing increasing efficiencies has become, to them, more a matter of "management by stress" than an understandable and rational policy. The ritualistic meetings, with their incantations to work hard and celebrate the company's spirit and mission, have a hollow ring. The promises about participation and opportunity seem empty.

One obvious effect of this malaise, as the Americans call it, is lower quality standards and lower productivity than the parent company in Japan is willing to tolerate. The American and Japanese managers know they have major problems, but neither side seems to know what to do about it. Several times during the past year, the American and Japanese managers have gotten together to work out issues at weekend retreats. Both sides worked hard at the process. Each time, a list of major problems was typed up and distributed to those in attendance. Each time, both sides vowed to push even harder to make the operation work. The following list was created at a recent retreat:

AMERICAN EXPECTATIONS OF SENIOR JAPANESE

1. Give open and honest information regarding targets, etc.
2. Recognize others—but only when justified.
3. Make Americans feel that they are part of the company.
4. Be consistent—treat Americans the same as the Japanese.
5. Tell Americans what you expect.
6. Don't imply. Don't be subtle. Be direct.
7. Don't speak Japanese without explaining.

1. Give your total commitment to the company's goals, especially in reaching two-year production targets because of their importance to worldwide plans and scale of investment.
2. Share the "burdens" of our situation (willingly accept criticism from Japan).
3. Try to communicate directly with Japan, using discretion.
4. Work together as an American team.
5. Accept overlapping/duplication of duties/responsibilities.

Did the list have a positive effect? "Within a week we are back where we started," says the human resources director. "It's not a matter of wanting to change. Both sides just talk past each other."

VISION AND VALUES

Japanese and North American organizations depend on commonly understood vision and values to give employees a sense of purpose and guide their behavior. Vision is the direction in which an organization is or should be heading. Vision is often expressed in a mission statement describing the nature of a company's business, products, services or market niches, how much growth is desired, the degree of reliance on new technology, and so forth. Vision establishes the reason an organization exists—what it hopes to accomplish, why these goals are important to employees, shareholders, customers, and, often, to society.

Values are guidelines that determine behavior in organizations. They guide everyday decision making by helping people understand what actions will help the organization live up to its vision. Some common values among North American organizations include continuous improvement, empowerment, exceeding customer expectations, and providing a balanced work life for employees. Together, vision and values form the culture of an organization.

Of the companies described, only the first company realized how important it was to have clearly understood vision and values. Before a single production worker was hired, Japanese and American managers spent time clarifying and refining the vision and values that would guide the new operation. They knew that much in the new operation would be unfamiliar and strange to North American workers, and that new employees would need some basic beliefs to help guide their actions and to understand the decisions and actions of American and Japanese management. To ensure that the vision and values would be understood, the managers were careful to work out behavioral examples illustrating how the vision and values would be applied in the workplace.

At the second Japanese operation, vision and values were basically imported wholesale from Japan. Little attention was given to making them relevant or understandable to a new type of employee in North America. Here and in other places, the roots of discord can be traced to a basic misunderstanding of a company's vision and values. If North Americans don't understand why decisions are made or why actions are taken, confusion and resentment often result.

Many of the values that lead to the success of Japanese companies, such as duty, obligation, and group loyalty, are deeply rooted in Japanese culture. Even so, Japanese companies do not assume that employees will automatically embrace company values. Just as Japanese society does, Japanese companies reinforce values in numerous ways. New managers and management trainees might attend "boot camps" where various initiation ceremonies bond them to the company. The only similar phenomena in North America are college fraternity and sorority "pledge weeks." In addition, uplifting company slogans, songs, and symbols help remind employees of basic organizational values. Values are constantly repeated in all types of communication and are modeled by supervisors and managers, who show by their own actions just how employees are expected to behave.

North American workers enter Japanese companies with different expectations. Their identification with their employer is not instantaneous; it will take years to build. This is illustrated by a survey conducted by the American magazine *Industry Week*,* in which Japanese and American workers were asked if they thought they would benefit personally from productivity improvements made by their employers. Ninety-three percent of Japanese respondents said yes; 91 percent of the Americans said no. While these data can be

---

* Modic, Stanley J. "Myths About Japanese Management." *Industry Week*, October 1987, pp. 49–53.

interpreted in several ways, it seems to us a further indication of a typical North American lack of identification with employers. Japanese respondents were unequivocal; they said that if productivity in the company goes up, they will benefit. Americans, on the other hand, expressed serious doubts about the relationship.

The lack of loyalty and sense of obligation that accompany low company identification can baffle Japanese managers in North America. *Kaizen* and similar concepts might be accepted by many North Americans, but not by all. Traditionally, continuous improvement has not been the responsibility of North American workers, who have felt that changes in production procedures, no matter how trivial, were best left to management. While increasing numbers of North Americans have embraced the notion of personal responsibility for continuous improvement, many, including many in management, still haven't gotten the message.

Our experience with Japanese start-ups in North America points to the need to pay a great deal of attention to developing a vision or mission statement and a set of values that reflect the purpose and objectives of a blended Japanese-North American organization. Often, a formal process works best. Participants in the process should include Japanese and North American managers. Many organizations have found that an off-site setting is the most appropriate place to conduct the process, which usually requires the help of outside consultants who specialize in helping organizations clarify vision and values.

The process is important because there is so much potential for vision and values to be misunderstood in a Japanese workplace in North America. Unfortunately, in our experience, Japanese managers often resist the idea of putting vision and values in writing, at least at first. While few Japanese managers are naive enough to assume that North American workers will immediately embrace company objectives, frequently they feel that other priorities are more important than developing clear vision and values. They hope that employees will come to understand the organization and their roles in it naturally. Later, however, Japanese managers usually agree with North American managers that the two or three days spent in vision and values clarification are among the most important periods in the start-up process.

There are numerous ways to develop a vision or mission statement and corresponding values. All require time, energy, and commitment. The mission statement usually is the easiest and can be very transferable from Japan. Defining appropriate values in ways that are easily understood and acted upon is more difficult.

Many North American organizations mistakenly ignore conflicts among values and try to instill too many values simultaneously. For example, we know of one pharmaceutical company with fourteen key values—not surprisingly, these values sometimes seem to contradict one another and paralyze performance rather than enhance it. Through a structured process, Japanese and North American managers together can identify a company's basic driving value and several supporting values. For most organizations, four to six values is a manageable number.

The mission and values of I/N Tek (Figure 5.1), a joint venture between Inland Steel and Nippon Steel, are good examples of what emerges from the close collaboration of Japanese and North American managers in the process of clarifying vision and values. Because of the need to check thoroughly for understanding and agreement at all levels of the organization, the process required several months to complete.

FIGURE 5.1
I/N TEK MISSION AND VALUES STATEMENT

MISSION

The I/N Tek mission is to produce the most marketable cold-reduced steel products sold in the United States, maintaining the highest standards in quality, cost, and consumer satisfaction through the integration of human resources, equipment, technology, and business systems, while providing secure and satisfying employment and an attractive return to investors.

VALUES

Quality Focus

We will commit our individual abilities and team efforts to achieve the highest-quality results in all aspects of the personal performance, the productive process, and all functions of the organization.

continued

Customer Orientation

We will seek out and satisfy our customers' needs and constantly strive to exceed their expectations. We recognize that the quality of our products has a powerful impact on our customers' manufacturing processes and the quality of their products.

Continuous Improvement (*Kaizen*)

We will continually strive to find better ways to do our work and to grow as individuals.

Participation and Involvement

We will seek input to find the best solutions to problems and methods of making improvements in the workplace. We will share information, resources, and ideas, and develop the skills necessary to maintain an exciting work environment where decisions are made at the lowest appropriate level.

People Focus

We will ensure a cooperative partnership among all members of I/N Tek in a framework built on mutual trust, respect, and a sense of dignity. We will provide opportunities for all employees to reach their maximum potential and experience more secure and satisfying employment in a safe and healthy environment.

Cost Consciousness

We will continually improve operating efficiency and reduce costs based on the recognition that every action we take can influence external as well as internal costs.

In addition to the definition of the values, behaviorally defined performance descriptions must be developed to support and illustrate the new values. Employees must understand not only the organization's values but also how their performance supports those values. Figure 5.2 shows how one organization defined two of its values.

FIGURE 5.2

EXAMPLE OF BEHAVIORAL DEFINITIONS THAT HELP EMPLOYEES
UNDERSTAND AND LIVE ACCORDING TO VALUES IN AN ORGANIZATION

MEETING CUSTOMER NEEDS

We seek to gain a clear understanding of our customers' personal and practical needs. We will take every step possible to exceed these needs, always striving to establish long-term, collaborative client relationships that are built on trust and mutual respect.

Importance

Because we represent a service business, the quality of our service will be our most important competitive advantage in the marketplace. In large measure, our success will be determined by how well we meet customer needs.

Practices

- Our interactions with clients will be based on the principles of honesty, integrity, and partnership.
- Our associates will be empowered to take actions to meet or exceed customer needs.
- We are dedicated to providing all associates with the skills and data needed to meet or exceed customer needs.
- Our top clients will receive extraordinary service because of an integrated team of personnel and our innovative approaches.
- We will continuously measure our customer satisfaction and, through constant improvement, strive to make our service even better in the future.
- Associates will be recognized and rewarded for their success in meeting or exceeding customer needs.

QUALITY OF LIFE FOR ASSOCIATES

Quality of life refers to an appropriate balance of work, play, family, and spiritual factors. We are committed to providing associates with stimulating and challenging work, while also allowing associates ample opportunity to balance that work with time for other activities.

continued

Importance

By showing our associates that we care about them as individuals, we foster commitment and loyalty to the company and our clients. We believe that caring is an inherent value of employment to which every associate is entitled.

Practices

- We will encourage and provide support for all associates to develop professionally and personally to the maximum of their capabilities.
- We will encourage and reinforce a balance in commitment between business and personal life.
- We will recognize that associates can have fun while fulfilling job responsibilities.
- We will search for ways to include family members in company functions and recognition events.
- We will value associates' differences and ideas, empowering them whenever possible.

Putting values into practice must be done through a carefully planned process. Part of the process involves developing training plans to make sure employees have the skills to support the organization's values. If participation is a value, for example, supervisors might need training in participative leadership skills. A fairly intensive assessment of organizational training needs is usually required to determine what training is needed to support the organization's values.

Communicating and reinforcing values must be a planned, ongoing process. For example, when people are promoted, it should be made clear that their promotions are the result of their adherence to the organization's values. When company plans are announced, they should be linked to the vision and values. Daily, ongoing operational decisions should reinforce values and, most important, not contradict or work against them. This requires a constant focus by top management on the organization's values and the impact of management decisions on the perception of those values. Management must model those values in everything it does. At every level, managers must show as well as tell subordinates that values are important.

The organization's compensation, appraisal, travel, and other systems must reinforce the company's values. Often North American workers think they receive one message from management and a very different message from important organizational systems. When this happens, they are more apt to believe that the system represents management's true values. For example, if flexibility and innovation are values, but the organization seems bogged down by endless bureaucratic procedures, it's easy to conclude that protecting bureaucratic fiefdoms is the true value, not flexibly responding to market opportunities.

How Good Are Japanese Managers at Communicating Vision and Values?

One Japanese manager with considerable experience in North America warns that Japanese companies often fail to understand the role of self-interest among local employees and the differences in expectations of its more heterogeneous workers. This includes those employees selected for their likelihood of thriving in the team-oriented, continuous productivity improvement environment of many Japanese organizations. Says this manager:

> Often the message communicated by Japanese management is some simple variation of "Be prompt and unquestioning every day, do good for the company and the company will do good for you and the world." That message needs to be balanced by the message that the organization exists to do good for the employees. And that's something that has to be shown by behavior and example.

Others caution that while the vision and values expressed by Japanese companies are "all high-sounding and impressive," as one American manager puts it, Japanese companies often fail to communicate how the vision and values actually work on a daily basis. "It all sounds great, but what does it mean day-to-day?"

These comments suggest that there is a wide gap between the stated vision and values of Japanese organizations in North America and perceived reality. Unfortunately, the wider the gap, the more damaging the effects on productivity and performance. North American managers frequently warn that their Japanese colleagues have to "walk like they talk." By that, they mean that after Japanese organizations communicate values to local employees, Japanese managers must be sure that their behavior and company policies do not contradict those values. For example, respect for individuals, participation, and teamwork can appear to be shallow, empty promises if local employees believe that personnel policies and management actions are arbitrary or petty.

When Japanese Companies Succeed

Often, the Japanese companies that have successfully instilled well-understood and accepted values in North America did so, in part, by sheer force of numbers. These companies imported many advisors, trainers, and production coordinators who clearly were animated by the vision and values of the company. Every day, local employees saw the focus and single-minded intensity of the Japanese personnel. "It's almost like osmosis," comments one American manager at a Japanese automaker. "The personal commitment and behavior required by *kaizen* and continuous productivity improvement just seep out."

Modeling organizational values is more difficult when the Japanese presence is small. In such cases, Japanese managers are forced to tell local employees about values rather than show them how values guide behavior. Because of poor communication skills and other factors, telling is often ineffective.

In Management Service Center of Japan's Overseas Managers program, which is designed to help Japanese managers prepare for North American assignments, one training exercise requires Japanese managers to prepare and present a speech that defines for a North American work group the vision and values of their organizations. Invariably, this exercise proves to be difficult and frustrating. Japanese managers usually are able to describe the values only in the most general terms—avoid waste, work cheerfully and productively every minute of every day, and so on. When they attempt to go beyond the generalities and describe how the values should guide behavior, Japanese managers have trouble putting them into words—especially English words. These same Japanese managers might feel that they understand their companies' values deeply and intuitively, but getting the ideas across in another language proves extraordinarily difficult. Japanese managers have little trouble describing steps or actions—

practice the "four whys" and the "six this or thats"—but what they are describing are not really values but methods to achieve the value of continuous improvement.

Once vision and values have been defined, it is relatively easy to train Japanese managers to communicate them effectively and to be able to relate common management decisions to those values. We suggest this step be accomplished as part of pretransfer language skills training. Vision and values offer a practical, job-related topic that can be dealt with at a number of language skill levels. What better area on which to focus some of the rote memorization that is part of language acquisition than an organization's vision and values?

Ultimately, clear vision and values, communicated and reinforced daily, are essential to creating empowered employees. Empowerment implies decision making by people lower in the organization, nearer to the work and the customers. To behave in an empowered fashion, employees need the guidance of vision and values. Without a complete understanding and deep commitment to an organization's vision and values, North Americans might never be able to make decisions on their own to the satisfaction of Japanese companies. As a result, decision making, by necessity, will remain in the hands of Japanese personnel, with headquarters maintaining tight, centralized control.

6

COMMUNICATING IN
THE WORKPLACE

You are always aware of how childlike you sound to Americans when you're required to use English. You think on a much higher level than you speak, but what can you do? You have to explain high-level concepts with simple words. It is a daily embarrassment. The Japanese hate to appear like fools.

JAPANESE MANAGER

A JAPANESE BURDEN

"WHEN WE WERE YOUNG, people my age never dreamed they'd be working in the United States," says a Japanese manager in his late forties. "It never occurred to us that learning to speak English well would be something we'd need later. Now we're here, and we're paying the price." The price he refers to is a daily, stressful battle to operate successfully in an English-language environment with sometimes only the most rudimentary ability to communicate with most of the other employees. Japanese managers in North America often resent the language burdens placed on them. "Americans working in Japan can usually do business in English," says one Japanese manager, "but in America, we are forced to use English." This manager acknowledges that English is the language of the international business world, but that doesn't overcome the resentment many Japanese managers feel. "It's not logical, but it's very emotional: Why is it always our side that must do business in a foreign language?"

It's definitely a lopsided situation, because few North Americans know Japanese and surprisingly few seem willing to learn. For example, most surveys show that fewer than one in twenty North American managers in Japanese organizations knows enough Japanese to converse with Japanese colleagues in their native tongue. Thus, the burden falls mainly to the Japanese, many of whom have at least a basic knowledge of written English. But most Japanese managers soon discover a huge difference between the written English needed to pass university entrance exams and the spoken English, with its various dialects and regional idiosyncrasies, encountered in North America.

The problem is becoming acute. When Japanese overseas investments were on a smaller scale, Japanese companies could get by with a limited number of overseas "specialists" fluent in local languages. Now, Japanese companies are forced to send dozens and sometimes hundreds of employees and managers to North America within short periods of time to start up or expand operations. For the most part, these are "ordinary" Japanese managers and employees with an ability to communicate in English that ranges from barely passable to virtually nonfunctional. Many of these same Japanese employees will be called upon to teach and train North Americans. Because of basic communication problems, this can be a disastrously inefficient process.

Many large Japanese companies have mounted intensive "crash" efforts to teach managers basic English skills, even for those assigned to Southeast Asia, Europe, and other overseas territories. But crash language programs can do only so much, and repeatedly, the communication difficulties between Japanese and North Americans become catalysts for numerous other problems. Often, the effort to use English becomes so difficult for Japanese managers that they begin to avoid situations in which English is needed. This tendency is understandable to many North Americans. For example, meetings that must be interrupted every few minutes for translation, or that seem to be composed of two competing groups—one speaking English, the other Japanese—are dreaded by everyone, especially if a delicate consensus must be forged out of the confusion. "If people hear a meeting is going to be translated, they simply won't go anymore," says an American in the Midwest, who adds that this seems perfectly acceptable to Japanese managers, inasmuch as they've started meeting among themselves anyway.

However, in North America and elsewhere, attempting to avoid the difficulties of communicating in English—whether through "Japanese-only" meetings or the designation of a few North American managers to serve as communication links between Japanese and native English-speaking personnel—puts unacceptable stress on the organization. For one thing, avoiding English contributes to the easily formed conviction of North American managers that a separate Japanese management channel is operating, independent of their involvement. "Because of language, we've got the Japanese reporting to Japanese, and in a parallel structure, Americans reporting to Americans," says an American manager. "And because of the difficulty of understanding one another, all the Americans are convinced that the separate Japanese-only hierarchy is running the show, and they're just standing on the sidelines."

This language gap can widen during times of pressure, according to many North Americans—for instance, when production goals aren't being met or when costs are running higher than anticipated. Unfortunately, these are situations in which the last thing an organization needs is deteriorating communications. "When something bad is going on, the Japanese revert to Japanese, leaving you out in the cold," complains an American manager. The result, he says, is a heightened sense of crisis and decreased morale among local employees.

SHOULD THE TABLES BE TURNED?

In the excitement over new jobs and local investment that often accompanies the opening of a Japanese operation in North America, new American employees often sign up en masse for Japanese-language classes, although few Japanese companies require or even suggest it. However, after confronting the reality of learning a difficult new language, the enthusiasm fades. In the first few months after the opening of a large Japanese manufacturing plant in the South, 300 local workers were studying Japanese. Two years later, only five

American workers were studying Japanese. At a six-year-old Japanese facility in the Midwest, plans to set up Japanese-language classes at a local junior college are still just plans. "We've got maybe ten people here out of 650 who are interested," says the American human resources manager. "We're waiting for a dozen and then we'll start a class. We've been waiting for about four years."

The situation is similar at other Japanese operations, where Japanese managers diligently try to improve their English skills while their North American colleagues either don't make the effort or take a few classes and conclude, "It's just too hard." At the employee level, North Americans in a Japanese production operation pick up a smattering of Japanese terms—*nemawashi, kaizen,* and others. Beyond that, little progress is made.

Is this enough? "It is doubtful that full integration of overseas executives in the management structure of the parent company is possible without some degree of familiarity with the Japanese language," concludes one recent study of Japanese operations in North America conducted by Egon Zehnder, an international executive recruiting firm. The study detected few signs of such integration happening anywhere. But rarely is this message delivered to North American managers, few of whom seem to understand that sharing the language of their parent firm might be one of the minimum requirements for the types of career opportunities they desire. Full integration, according to the study's authors, would include regular (not training) assignments for local managers at Japanese headquarters. Currently, this is virtually nonexistent and is not likely to happen soon without more effort by local managers to develop Japanese-language skills.*

North American companies operating overseas routinely require local employees to learn English. It is quickly understood that advancement for local employees, even into first-level supervision, requires minimal English fluency; advancement into management requires considerable fluency—this, despite the fact that North American managers themselves are usually satisfied with only a superficial ability to speak the language of their host countries.

* *Management Culture and the Effectiveness of Local Executives in Japanese-Owned U.S. Corporations.* Egon Zehnder International Tokyo/The University of Michigan, 1990, pp. 13–15.

Should Japanese organizations make the same demands? Logically, perhaps yes, but Japanese companies have been understandably reluctant to ask North American managers to study Japanese. For one thing, such a requirement could seriously hamper recruitment efforts. It also might require some creative incentives, given the laziness of North Americans when it comes to learning foreign languages. Realistically, few North Americans are likely to learn enough Japanese to become truly effective communicators in Japanese. But, encouraging or, in some cases, requiring local managers to study Japanese can have other effects. For one thing, trying to learn Japanese would make local managers better communicators in a multilingual environment. They would become sensitive to the challenge of conveying meaning and detail. They also would likely become more innovative and resourceful at devising methods to alleviate the special communication problems that arise in the Japanese-North American workplace. At the very least, local managers would be more understanding of the difficulties facing Japanese managers forced to speak English.

Here's how one Japanese manager puts it:

Why is it important that Americans try to learn Japanese? They may not advance beyond the most basic level, but they'll learn how hard it is to speak in a foreign language. They'll learn the patience, which most now do not have, to listen to poor English. Otherwise, they take speaking English for granted. They hear Japanese using English and think to themselves, "Why, even four-year-olds speak better than that." If they understand the difficulties, it makes understanding much easier.

As Japanese and North American managers make consistent and frequent efforts to help one another acquire the other's native language, another thing happens: The shared challenge gives Japanese and North Americans something real and very tangible in common, and it builds a bond of cooperation and trust.

THE TROUBLE WITH *WA*

There's a difference between knowing a foreign language and being able to communicate in that language.

American working in Tokyo

There are nine ways to say "yes" in Japanese. But none of them mean "yes."

> Owner of an Ohio parts
> supplier to a Japanese
> automaker

If you want to get along in the world, say "Yes, that's true" and "That's very reasonable; there's nothing especially difficult about it." . . . If you don't want to get along in the world, say "That isn't so" and "Yes, but . . ." This is not what is wanted; it is unexpected.

> MORINOBU NEGISHI
> (1737–1815), author,
> *Mimibukro*

The North American manager who has taken the time to read about Japanese culture is familiar with the social importance of *wa* (wǎ), or harmony. *Wa* is maintained by balancing *tatemae* (tǎ-tǎ-mǎ-ā), one's official stance on a matter, and *honne* (hōn-nay), one's true feelings or intentions. Along with *tatemae* and *honne*, such a North American also might tell you about *omote* (ōmō-tay), which is the outward, superficial appearance which one displays, and *ura* (oo-rǎ), the hidden implications of one's behavior. Unfortunately, this sensitive and complex Japanese style of communicating can create confusion in North American operations, where local employees might need clarity far more than they need subtlety and discretion.

Clifford Clarke, an American consultant to Japanese organizations, has noted that, "To many Americans, being honest about one's feelings is a measure of integrity. To many Japanese, integrity is manifested in virtually the opposite fashion—by behaving harmoniously and adjusting to the feelings of others. If you don't maintain harmony, you're self-centered, a bad influence, lacking integrity."* A Japanese manager sees it similarly. "In the U.S., people place great emphasis on being what they call true to themselves. They think integrity involves insisting on one's beliefs or opinions and persuading others. In Japan, integrity involves mutually making concessions and looking for a

---

* Clarke, C. "East Meets West: An Interview with Clifford Clarke." *Training and Development Journal*, October 1990, pp. 43–47.

basis for compromise. Instead of trying to persuade others, you adapt yourself to others."

Many Americans seem to think that most communication problems in the Japanese-North American workplace could be solved if Japanese employees were trained to be more direct in a supposedly American fashion. However, many Japanese, especially older and more traditional Japanese, would see this as training in being disrespectful or training in how to violate harmony—an attempt, in other words, to erase a lifetime of observance of cultural rules.

Clear communication is a big issue with Westerners working in Japan as well. There, North Americans often complain that even those Japanese professionals whose jobs require them to give opinions, such as lawyers and accountants, provide vague, highly qualified answers that are sometimes impossible to decipher and that render their responses useless. "Japan is a society of conjecture," says a Japanese executive, trying to explain some of the difficulties Westerners encounter when seeking straightforward, unequivocal answers. "From childhood, the Japanese receive daily training on how to judge correctly the intentions of others and the situations they are in. This training teaches them when to ask questions and when to refrain from asking questions, when to answer and when to offer vague responses."

North Americans often call this speaking in "shades of gray" versus speaking in "black and white," and say it is among the most confusing aspects of Japanese communication. Even the most fluent and astute Western speakers of Japanese must constantly be sensitive to a rich, multilayered hierarchy of nuance, subtlety, and meaning in the Japanese language. But that creates an immense challenge in North America: How do you integrate the values of Japanese-style harmony—which places a premium on avoiding confrontation, requires that positions and feelings often be stated indirectly, and can easily lead insensitive listeners to draw wrong conclusions—with a more North American approach that tends to be direct, verbal, analytical, and sometimes confrontational?

The challenge can be seen in even the most basic forms of communication. For example, many North Americans find that Japanese colleagues are reluctant to provide simple yes or no answers. Or, if they do answer, they do so in such an excessively qualified and often convoluted manner that the listener is more confused than enlightened. "Did he say 'no'? Or did he say 'yes' and mean 'no'? You have to ask yourself that question every day here," says an American manager in California, who adds that when North Americans are forced to guess at the intentions of Japanese colleagues, they often guess incorrectly.

One simple difference in communication patterns that proves surprisingly difficult for both Japanese and North Americans is how each side answers "yes" or "no." In Japanese speech, answering a question, such as "Didn't you know the fact that . . . ?" requires an answer of either "Yes, I didn't," or "No, I did." The Western response is the reverse: "No, I didn't," or "Yes, I did." These distinct patterns are so ingrained in Japanese and North Americans that both often say they have to hesitate before answering even the simplest "yes" or "no" question in the other's language. Even after many months of study, Western students of the Japanese language find this difficult. Likewise, Japanese learners say this is one of the most confusing aspects of English. It's only one example, however, of how the basic structures of both languages differ and why communication in Japanese or English can be so hard.

Other differences go beyond words. Studies in cross-cultural communication, for example, show that Japanese expatriate managers listen with twice the rate of head-nodding as Western managers. Along with the head-nodding, a Japanese manager will frequently say "yes, yes." To North Americans, such behavior ordinarily signifies comprehension. If it's not followed by objections or other instructions, it also might signal approval. However, it often means merely that, "I'm listening, please continue"—an early lesson for many North Americans in Japanese organizations.

North Americans also note that Japanese colleagues are reluctant to express opinions and take stands on issues. Instead, they respond situationally. "They read the situation and then tell you whatever it is they think you want to hear," one American manager says. "That could involve changing previously stated answers and responses to meet the needs of the moment or avoid what could potentially be a conflict. It's extremely confusing."

It's worth noting that Japanese and North Americans find much to admire in one another's communication styles, even when those styles lead to confusion or conflict. Japanese who work with North Americans in Japan often comment on how disruptive they find the blunt and aggressive manners of North Americans, but at the same time they admit that the Japanese could learn a few lessons. "Their willingness to express opinions clearly and frankly, even to their bosses, even when they might be in opposition to what others think, helps them clarify issues and move ahead," says a Japanese manager in the Tokyo office of an American computer company. "Perhaps the biggest difference between us and them is that they don't suffer from the perception that expressing opinions leads to ill feelings in other activities or personal affairs." On the other hand, North Americans often admire how the Japanese style of communication, with its emphasis on observing hierarchical relationships and group harmony, strengthens the organization.

In North America, however, Japanese communication patterns can lead to mistakes, missed deadlines and, as one American manager puts it, "daily slips and screwups and running around checking with second and third parties with questions like 'Did I hear him right?' 'What did he tell you he thought I said?' and 'What do you think he really meant?'" What makes the confusion so bad, this manager says, is the resentment it generates among local employees when they are criticized for doing things they thought had been approved or at least acknowledged by Japanese personnel.

Many North Americans fail to realize that Japanese managers often do not communicate more clearly simply because of their limited command of English. For many Japanese, spoken English can be a monumentally difficult language to master. One reason might be the relative lack of emphasis the Japanese educational system places on conversational English. It has been noted that, even with their native language, the Japanese place a much greater emphasis on the written word than the spoken word. Americans teaching English to the Japanese have noted that in Japan the reason typically given for studying a foreign language is to learn how to read and write it—not necessarily how to speak it.

Besides, the Japanese language, virtually unique among the world's 3,000 languages, provides little useful foundation for learning to speak a language such as English. English has limitations when it comes to expressing relationships, especially those based on age and hierarchies. Many Japanese managers say this makes it difficult to ask questions or probe for information in English without appearing rude or causing offense. Thus, Japanese trying to learn to use English as North Americans do must overcome several important aspects of their upbringing and culture. This not only leads to difficulty in communicating in an English-speaking environment but also to the resentment many Japanese feel toward North Americans, who seem not to appreciate this struggle.

TONGUE-TIED GIANTS

Edwin Reischauer, a former U.S. ambassador to Japan, has called the Japanese a race of "tongue-tied giants." To Reischauer, the Japanese are highly ambivalent about spoken language. Using words is just one of several ways to communicate, and sometimes words are inappropriate.* North Americans, encouraged to "spill their guts" from childhood, often have difficulty understanding this notion. It might sound simplistic, but observers of the two cultures say the Japanese just aren't as talkative as Americans. Writing in *The New York Times,* Masao Kunihiro, a newscaster and member of the Japanese Diet, put it this way:

> The Japanese have come to look upon language in general with a jaundiced eye, as both insufficient and incomplete. Whatever value language has for the communication of knowledge and facts, when it comes to the mutual expression of deep thoughts and feelings, nonverbal communication is far more crucial and effective.†

Kunihiro cites research showing that the Japanese spend four hours a day in verbal communication, while Americans spend eight. The Japanese language itself contains many proverbs that express contempt for loquacity and eloquence. A recent survey in Japan showed that 76 percent of the Japanese thought a taciturn man would be more successful in business than a garrulous one. No one has asked North Americans the same question, but the response probably would be just the opposite. To North Americans, fast, glib speech is an important part of successful deal making and business negotiating. Kunihiro goes on to say this about the Japanese: "To expect a people

* Reischauer, E. *The Japanese.* Harvard University Press, 1977, pp. 135–137.

† Kunihiro, M. "Why the Japanese Talk English Bad." *New York Times,* May 9, 1991, pp. 13–15.

that feels this negatively about self-expression to master a foreign language, particularly a spoken foreign language, is like climbing a tree in search of fish."

"Like nature, Americans abhor a vacuum when it comes to talking," says a Japanese advisor in the U.S. Northeast. "Gaps in conversation make them uncomfortable. You have to learn how to fill up the gaps with small talk and chatter." Other Japanese observers agree that North Americans seem to have an insatiable appetite for the sound of their own voices. To Japanese managers, it might seem that nowhere is this dependence on verbal communication more apparent than the workplace. Here, North Americans prize expressing their opinions frequently and, sometimes, to anyone who will listen. Praise, flattery, cajolery, and a steady stream of words seem to be an important part of a North American manager's arsenal of people-management skills.

"Americans are not well trained to use silence as a constructive part of interpersonal relations," says Clifford Clarke. "We have a taboo against silence and will rush to fill the void as if silence were a negative, a kind of emptiness."* Silence to the Japanese is just the opposite; Japanese culture attributes great importance to the pregnant pause and contemplative silence. Those who seem incapable of using silence risk being associated with such undesirable qualities as impatience and thoughtlessness, or worse, having something to hide.

North Americans living in Japan often become quite comfortable with the use of silence as a way to convey meaning. "When you return to America," says one, "you notice the difference immediately. Americans just don't seem to be able to shut up. The continuous talk makes them seem like they are trying to cover up something." Americans also learn that many Japanese consider English spoken rapidly as showing off. Americans who work under senior and respected Japanese managers and executives also learn that in high positions, deliberate and stately speech is expected. People who talk fast lose dignity. In many ways, the exact opposite is true of top North American managers and executives.

North Americans are sometimes confused by the lengthy pauses and bowed heads of Japanese managers considering replies to questions. The North Americans see this as a lack of comprehension and

---

* Clarke, C. "East Meets West: An Interview with Clifford Clarke." *Training and Development Journal*, October 1990, pp. 43–47.

hurriedly restate the question rather than wait for a response. To North Americans, it is important to fill in the gap with more words. Japanese managers sometimes leave a sentence unfinished for the listener to complete. This habit also can thoroughly confuse the North American listener; to the Japanese manager, it's a use of silence that avoids expressing an idea before discovering how the listener feels about it.

To North Americans, Japanese colleagues can be harder to "read" because of their relative lack of facial expression. North Americans frequently say that their Japanese colleagues seem to reserve certain facial expressions for exclusive use among themselves. With North Americans, the Japanese manager's repertoire seems to be limited to two facial expressions—smiling and blank. North Americans suggest that this stems primarily from Japanese managers' belief that there is some risk of others "losing face" when emotions are visible. Consequently, gestures or expressions that might indicate emotional state often are so well masked as to be imperceptible. The absence of such cues, so important to North Americans, can be bewildering.

CHECKING FOR UNDERSTANDING

These and other basic differences in communication patterns, as well as the great disparities in English skills among Japanese managers, mean that checking for understanding is often the primary day-to-day challenge in the Japanese workplace in North America. Various strategies are adopted by North American managers, mostly involving keeping records of nearly *everything*. The purpose is to have some form of documentation when questions inevitably arise about what Japanese managers said—and what they meant by what they said. Gathering documentation can be time-consuming and cumbersome, but as one American manager says, "It's the only way to really protect yourself." Another manager describes his approach:

> After about a year, one gets used to the habit of the Japanese holding simultaneous meetings in their own language. It used to bother me, but now it bothers me if they don't discuss things in Japanese, as it indicates that they don't understand. The subtlety of the Japanese in expressing disagreement is a problem, but I find that if I am in any doubt as to the

outcome of a meeting, I make sure that I summarize it in writing and make clear what I believe to have been decided and give the Japanese time to object if necessary before implementing the decisions.

To help in documentation, many organizations install electronic copy boards in meeting rooms and production areas so that informal diagrams and jottings made during meetings can be recorded and kept for future reference.

Documenting decisions is a new idea to the Japanese and takes them some time to get used to. Some Japanese managers suggest that this diligence for keeping written records is peculiar to Western business practice, and that it is unnecessary and even counterproductive in organizations based on Japanese management. "When decisions are dictated and not made through consensus, as in American companies, keeping records might be needed for self-preservation and keeping things straight," says a Japanese manager. "But it might be better to take the time to meet until a consensus that everyone agrees to and understands is reached. Then people don't need records to know what they have to do." Others suggest that the Japanese managers' flexibility in responding to changing situations would be limited if they were forced to commit to certain actions in writing.

Many North Americans say that Japanese managers dislike paper trails. A paper trail runs counter to the Japanese disdain for memos and written records. But what works in Japan does not necessarily work in North America. North American managers feel compelled to aggressively track and record daily interactions. Otherwise, the likelihood of Japanese and North American misinterpretation is simply too great. "In a Japanese company, you need to learn how to *overcommunicate* before you can start to communicate," says one American manager.

The process of learning to communicate can be agonizingly slow. In the opinion of many North Americans, a North American setting seems to pose so many potential dangers to Japanese managers that they remain excessively polite and superficial communicators throughout their assignments. The Japanese, not wanting to confuse, offend, or cause others to lose face, are unwilling to be direct and honest or to state positions and opinions in ways that provide useful feedback. Because Japanese managers are frequently reassigned, the process of establishing good working relationships based on meaningful communication is often aborted before it has a chance to get started. This makes it easy to mistake behavior based on deep cultural differences and a lack of training in cross-cultural communication skills for something completely different—a deliberate policy of exclusion and discrimination.

TRANSLATORS

Experienced Japanese and North American managers cite the importance of hiring language experts with a good cultural and colloquial understanding of Japanese and English. "Mediocre interpreters abound," one Japanese manager warns. Many Japanese managers need a confidant who understands American culture and its values and can filter and modify their messages when they run the risk of confusing or alienating people. Japanese companies can especially benefit from individuals who can translate peculiar Japanese themes (as in mission statements, philosophies, and statements of values) into terms North Americans find relevant.

JAPANESE CULTURAL VALUES THAT HAVE AN IMPACT ON VERBAL COMMUNICATION

- Silence is golden.
- Smooth talkers are not trusted.
- The fewer words, the better.
- The subject of the sentence can be understood without stating it.
- It is impolite to address people of higher status by name.
- It is effective to cite past examples to persuade others.
- It is risky to be assertive.
- Saying "no" destroys human relationships.
- Intonation and tone tell more than the words themselves.
- It is good to rely on one's intuition and feelings.
- It is rude to ask questions.

Adapted from a presentation by Mrs. Miyo Umeshima of Management Service Center Company, Ltd., Japan, 1992.

7

MEETINGS:

WHERE DIFFERENCES RISE TO THE SURFACE

We make progress. We start working as a team. We start getting around our differences. Then we have a meeting and we all realize how far apart we really are.

AMERICAN MANAGER

ASK A TYPICAL North American manager what he dislikes most about life inside a Japanese-run company, and you're likely to get a simple answer: meetings. Most North Americans understand the necessity of frequent meetings in new or expanding operations. Most realize that the process of coordinating local and Japanese employees requires intensive face-to-face contacts and numerous conferences, big and small. Few North Americans, however, easily adjust to the very different orientation Japanese organizations have toward meetings. This problem is due in part to the tedious struggle to overcome communication difficulties. However, the primary cause might be the different roles meetings play in Japanese and North American business culture.

To start, meetings illustrate some of the more difficult aspects of consensus-style operations for North Americans, who persist in feeling that while the consensus process isn't entirely democratic, it *is* supposed to be participatory. "Consensus is not a debate followed by a vote; we know that," says one U.S. manager:

> We also know it's not a compromise between opposing points of view— you can't manage by committee. But we understood the system to mean that you're willing to argue a point while at the same time you're willing to be convinced. From all these points of view, an intelligent decision emerges that everyone supports. If no consensus emerges, then, of course, someone has to decide unilaterally, but at least he has everyone's viewpoint to consider. But we didn't think it meant you're supposed to sit and sit and sit until you smile and agree with the boss. But that seems to happen when a plan is laid on the table, supposedly open for discussion, and it really isn't. . . .

Other North American managers maintain that the Japanese place such a heavy emphasis on the *appearance* of consensus that they go to elaborate—and transparent—lengths to get North Americans to support decisions, as though they actually had a part in reaching them. It's a feeble way, these managers say, of building a sense of ownership and commitment. "It makes you feel that they aren't interested in what we think at all," says one American manager. Says another:

> The Japanese have their staff meetings on Monday afternoons. Then we have our daily production meetings with key Japanese people. A lot gets lost about how and why things are being done. It's a fairly universal feeling among the Americans that the real decisions are made at those Monday meetings. When we meet with the Japanese, sometimes we're just going through the motions, since it's apparent that a decision has already been made. I manage to keep a sense of humor, but not everyone can laugh it off. A lot of team and unit leaders will say later, "Why don't they tell us what they want us to do? Why do they make us jump through these hoops?" You go through this entire process of discussing an issue that was decided on before the meeting began. People resent it. They're not so stupid that they don't see through the charade.

Another American calls it an attempt to "manipulate reality" when a meeting is held to discuss a topic on which a decision has already been reached. "They are trying to create the appearance of genuine agreement or harmony among the Japanese and Americans in a phony discussion. It's all very unreal," says the manager.

But such meetings are no charade to the Japanese organization. The Japanese hold frequent meetings to give employees the chance to understand and emotionally commit to policies and decisions they will be expected to implement. Meetings play a major role in keeping communication flowing. With less emphasis on formal controls and written memoranda, meetings in Japanese organizations provide opportunities that might not exist otherwise; in these meetings, team members learn what's going on in their own and other work areas. Meetings also give managers the chance to check on the status of projects in a nonconfrontational way.

As one Japanese manager puts it:

During meetings you gather information about your company, however trivial it seems, and however unrelated to your present job. Japanese management trainees know they will be rotated from one section to another, accumulating experiences from various jobs, and a broad company knowledge is essential. Managers also need these meetings, since they are expected to have a broad view and know everything about the company. You need the ability to guess or sense the direction and atmosphere of the company. In order to make a correct judgment, ample information is important, and information gathering is a necessary practice. Meetings provide the opportunities.

North American managers estimate that Japanese organizations conduct two to three times as many meetings as North American organizations of a similar size and nature. "You meet and meet and meet, and half the time you don't know why," complains an American manager. Communication difficulties, especially when translation is needed, make meetings even more vexing. "Every twenty-minute meeting takes about two hours," says another manager. "I thought I was hired to help get production going, not to spend 75 percent of my time in meetings."

The inclusion of nearly everyone who might be affected, no matter how remotely, by policies or decisions discussed during meetings also can lead to boredom and inattention among North Americans. "From the Japanese perspective, if you're there, you've bought into whatever decisions are reached," says an American manager. "Even if it doesn't affect you now, it could at some point. And if it does, you've already bought into it. That makes sense in a way," this manager says, "but the problem is that just about *everything* can ultimately affect you—and we meet on just about everything." As a result, the content of meetings sometimes seems so unrelated to their duties and responsibilities that North American managers do not understand why they're expected to be in a particular meeting, or what they are expected to do with the information that emerges from it.

Other aspects of the Japanese meeting style prove equally hard to get used to. Open office areas, already distracting to many local managers, "encourage a huddle on every play," says one American manager, using a football analogy to describe meetings on matters that he thinks are too minor to require the disruption of work routines. In addition to believing that meetings are called too spontaneously and too frequently, North Americans say that Japanese managers use meetings to "fish" indiscriminately for information.

Cultural differences in communication are very apparent during meetings in Japanese organizations in North America. North Americans want to debate points and "hammer" out a compromise. Disagreement is acceptable as long as it is presented objectively. Opposing viewpoints can be debated—and rejected—without risking open warfare. Clarity and directness are valued, while formalities and face-saving gestures are considered less important. The purpose is to get to the point and get the meeting over with as quickly as possible.

Japanese managers, on the other hand, may adopt a more indirect, potentially less confrontational stance during meetings, typically soliciting information from others without revealing their own feelings. Their style can confuse and frustrate North Americans. "They talk around and around a subject to get everyone's point of view, so carefully avoiding anything that might provoke disagreement or confrontation that you hardly ever know what's on their minds," says an American manager. The result, this manager says, is a kind of communication gridlock. "You're always in doubt about what the Japanese are really after. Frequently you don't understand the intent of their questions, or appreciate the effect of your responses. It takes forever to get to the point or really focus on exactly what it is they're trying to say. You can't really contribute much until you figure it out." Other North American managers chafe at the unusual (for North Americans) level of sensitivity and tact required during meetings in Japanese organizations. "Frankly, it makes it difficult to discuss problems," a North American manager says. "Sometimes it makes discussing problems that need to be discussed an activity that all sides avoid. Because we're all so delicate with one another during meetings, we have a tendency to lurch from crisis to crisis. When you need action, you don't get it until it's twice as hard to fix."

If one thing crystallizes the difference between North American and Japanese feelings about meetings, it's the tendency of some Japanese managers to sleep during meetings. This behavior surprises and even shocks North Americans, who find anything less than complete alertness during meetings inappropriate. Of course, North American managers realize that language difficulties require Japanese participants to focus intensely on what's being said in English. The result is often a meditative posture that can be mistaken for sleeping. In fact, Japanese managers often do sleep during meetings. Americans in Japan note that sleep deprivation, overwork, and, not infrequently, being hung over (from social/business drinking the night before) are so common that sleeping in public places—on the train, at a lecture or concert, even during a business meeting—is not considered unusual. But to North Americans, with their "let's-get-to-the-point-and-get-out-of-here-quickly" attitudes toward meetings, sleeping during a meeting seems ludicrous and comic—or would be if it weren't so frustrating. "Because you have enough on the agenda for four or five separate meetings among four or five different groups, various Japanese managers seem to be able to tune out at will," complains an American manager. "They snap back into consciousness when matters concerning them come up, and then tune out again when they don't have to listen anymore. Meanwhile, you're sitting there worrying about whether you'll have enough time left after the meeting to get back to the pile of work on your desk."

PRESCRIPTION: FINDING COMMON GROUND

There are ways to make meetings more productive and less frustrating to North American managers and still accomplish the objectives of Japanese managers. Development of the meeting leadership skills of the Japanese and North Americans is required. In the box that follows we describe the skills that should be developed.

MEETING LEADERSHIP SKILLS

DETERMINE IF A MEETING IS NECESSARY AND WHO SHOULD ATTEND

Before planning or calling a meeting, Japanese managers need to consider two issues:

1. *Is it necessary?* With their meetings-as-a-last-resort mentality, North American managers think that other methods of communication are more efficient—a memorandum, for instance, or a one-on-one discussion. The big question North American managers ask when contemplating a meeting is: *Do the benefits of having a meeting outweigh other options?*

"Memos and reports might be more efficient. In meetings, everyone's got to sound off on stuff you probably already know, don't need to know, or could have scanned in a second or two in a memo," says an American manager. But Japanese managers disagree. For them, memos merely provide excuses for inaction, and relying on memos and written reports can run counter to the spirit of true consensus-style management, which involves discussions and comments from many people. Memos and reports would have to be revised continuously if they really reflected the dynamics of the process. More likely, they would impose constraints on the process. Besides, meeting frequently, even on the spur of the moment, provokes the maximum flow of information within work groups and organizations.

Both views hold valid points. Clearly, overreliance on either meetings or memos is inappropriate. Both should be used depending on what is to be accomplished.

2. *Who should attend?* One North American manager estimates that half the meetings he attends at his Japanese company leave him wondering, *Why am I here?* His dilemma seems typical. Whatever the merits of including as many participants as possible in meetings, the approach inevitably causes frustration for North Americans. North American managers contend that participants in a meeting should have some contribution to make, information to provide, and/or some recognizable stake in the outcome of the meeting.

continued

DEFINE AND COMMUNICATE THE PURPOSE AND IMPORTANCE OF THE MEETING

Typically, in North American organizations, meetings have one or more purposes, which usually fall into these five categories:

1. Problem solving
2. Clarifying/Informational
3. Brainstorming
4. Progress reports
5. Progress review

Similar types of meetings are held, of course, in purely Japanese organizations. A crucial difference, though, is that in North American organizations, the category of meeting usually is communicated ahead of time. In this way, managers know how to prepare, what to expect, and how to respond during a meeting.

• In *problem-solving meetings,* the purpose is to agree on solutions and decide on specific actions to solve a problem. Examples include finding the source of a quality problem and determining the most appropriate staffing for a new project.

• In *clarifying/informational meetings,* the purpose is to communicate information about changes or decisions affecting a specific work group. Information is provided by the meeting leader or group members. Typically, no action or decision is required. Examples include meetings on safety and introducing changes within the organization.

• In *brainstorming meetings,* the purpose is to generate a number of ideas or solutions without criticism or evaluation. No specific action or decision is required. Later these ideas or solutions will be used by the same group members or others to reach final decisions. Examples include meetings on productivity improvement, new product ideas, and exploring opportunities for change.

• *Progress report meetings* allow group members to update others on the status of projects or work in progress. This type of session is intended to give information; it is not meant to be an open forum.

continued

Examples include annual, quarterly, monthly, or weekly reports; and task force and special-project team reports.

• In *progress review meetings*, information is given by one group member. A progress review differs from a progress report in that once the information is given, it is analyzed and discussed by other group members. Aside from giving information, the primary purpose of this kind of meeting is to solicit suggestions or feedback. Usually in this type of meeting no specific action is taken. Examples include budget meetings and long- and short-range planning sessions.

To North Americans, the purpose of a meeting in a Japanese organization often is unidentifiable. Managers might enter what they think is one type of meeting and learn (or suspect) as the meeting progresses that the intention is quite different. A prime example is a problem-solving meeting that turns into a clarifying/informational meeting. The "discussion" of a problem really serves to camouflage the announcement of a decision.

PROVIDE AGENDAS

To North American managers, an agenda communicates the purpose of a meeting; further, it serves as a tool to help accomplish a meeting's objectives within the allotted time. Without agendas, meetings can drift aimlessly, leaving North American participants wondering if anything actually was accomplished.

Agendas have a unique advantage for North Americans working in Japanese organizations—they help overcome communication problems. One American manager distributes a detailed agenda to Japanese staff a day or so ahead of an important meeting, summarizing the main points to be discussed. Virtually all Japanese read English well and having the opportunity to study an agenda ahead of the meeting means at the very least that they are usually well prepared at the meeting. It also reduces the number of occasions that the Japanese staff revert to separate meetings in their own language.

For a Japanese manager with shaky presentation skills and limited English-speaking ability, a written agenda can be an important aid to communicating more effectively. An agenda anchors and focuses a speaker's remarks by giving the speaker and the participants some-

continued

thing to refer back to as points are made. An agenda also can serve as an aid to checking for understanding by helping the speaker ensure that essential points are understood before moving on.

Certainly, the use of agendas is not a foreign concept for the Japanese. The difference is that, while agendas are used more widely in conferences and large presentations in Japan than in the United States, they aren't used as much in small meetings—particularly spontaneous meetings like the ones occurring frequently in Japanese-owned companies in North America.

PRACTICE MEETING LEADERSHIP SKILLS

Once a meeting is deemed appropriate, effective meeting leadership plays an important role in keeping a meeting productive and on track. When people meet, someone has to be in charge, however nominally. Leadership can be retained by one person throughout the meeting, or shared as the meeting moves from one topic to another. Meeting leadership is a skill North Americans sometimes find lacking in their Japanese colleagues—or is practiced so invisibly that it seems to be lacking. The reasons, North American managers speculate, might be an unwillingness on the part of many Japanese managers to risk the appearance of being domineering or discouraging others' participation.

The skills of effective meeting leadership, however, are not inconsistent with conducting a Japanese-style meeting. In fact, in many ways they parallel the inclination of Japanese managers to give individuals as much leeway as possible. One meeting leadership training program used by many U.S. corporations takes a critical steps approach to conducting meetings effectively. These critical steps require a direct (but nonconfrontational) style that might seem difficult for some Japanese managers to master. However, the effort is important because these steps can help prevent meetings from deteriorating into aimless and time-consuming exercises in futility for North American managers.

As you will see, many of the critical steps represent areas in which North Americans believe most Japanese managers are sorely deficient.

continued

FOLLOW THE CRITICAL STEPS*

Following the critical steps outlined here will ensure that meetings are productive for all participants—North Americans and Japanese alike.

• **Explain the purpose and importance of the meeting.** The purpose is a concise statement of objectives to be achieved during the meeting. It answers the questions, "Why is this meeting taking place?" and "Why is the discussion important to me and the organization?" As we've seen, both pieces of information are vital to North American participants.

By explaining the type of meeting and its relevance to group members, you will encourage cooperation and help participants understand their valuable role in the meeting's success. This approach also provides an opportunity for you to maintain or enhance self-esteem within the group.

• **Review agenda.** An agenda is more than a mere list of topics to be discussed. It is a way of making sure the meeting is productive. The agenda also outlines the procedures you want to follow in discussing the topics. If you distribute the agenda in advance, open the meeting by briefly reviewing the procedures to be followed, as well as the sequence of topics.

When appropriate, indicate how much time is allotted for each item on the agenda. Because it is important to gain the group's acceptance and support for the agenda, ask if anything needs to be added or deleted and answer any questions.

If no agenda has been prepared before the meeting, use a flip chart to outline the agenda at the beginning of the meeting. Then, check for agreement before proceeding. This is a good way to show that you are open to the group's ideas.

• **Collect and clarify relevant information.** For each topic, point out all relevant information and check for understanding. Participants often will want to generate solutions or decide on courses of action prematurely. Listen empathetically to their thoughts and ideas, and explain the importance of reviewing each situation thoroughly before moving on to problem solving or action planning.

* These critical steps are part of Development Dimensions International's Meeting Leadership and Team Action[sm] programs. Copyright © 1990 by Development Dimensions International, Inc. World rights reserved.

continued

If any constraints or suggestions are proposed at the meeting, consider them immediately. If you have information from previous meetings or other sources that is unknown to the rest of the group, introduce it and ask about any concerns regarding the information. As we have seen, North Americans hate to feel that important information is being withheld from them.

• **Summarize the information discussed.** You'll need to determine at which point to end the collection of relevant information and begin a summary (a brief overview of what's been covered). Your summary will help ensure that everyone has the same understanding before solutions or alternatives are sought.

If the issues are complex, you can review content or further clarify information. If the discussion has been fairly straightforward, your summary will serve as a transition point to the next step. A good summary should be concise. Summarizing information helps to allay some of the frustration North Americans feel in an unstructured, meandering meeting.

• **Seek suggestions, solutions, or alternatives.** Involve the group in developing suggestions, solutions, or alternatives. In this way, you will encourage cooperation in reaching your stated objective. People are more willing to commit to solutions they have helped to develop. Seeking suggestions also is an effective way to enhance the self-esteem of all participants; this, in turn, increases their commitment even more.

• **Reach agreement on specific action(s).** It is important for a group to agree on specific actions and responsibilities. To ensure agreement, summarize the information and check for understanding. This will increase the group's level of commitment. Whenever appropriate, allow participants to choose specific actions or assignments.

Specify who is responsible for what and by when. Regardless of how successful the discussion seems, North American participants will not see the value of the meeting if they leave it feeling unsure of specific actions and responsibilities.

• **Summarize and set follow-up dates.** A concise summary of agreements reached, specific actions to be taken, and responsibilities assigned will ensure that everyone understands what is to be done. Setting follow-up dates emphasizes the importance of decisions made. Follow-up lets you or the group check progress and ensure that nothing is overlooked.

continued

Successful meeting leadership requires mastery of a number of "process" skills. Foremost is checking for understanding. This is often the most important, yet perplexing, requirement in a meeting between Japanese and North Americans. Using this skill ensures that all meeting participants are, at least, considering the same information and understand each other's point of view.

Many Japanese-North American organizations have learned from experience to use charts and diagrams when checking for understanding. Japanese managers are very accomplished in using simple models or diagrams to convey complex issues. This use of visual aids helps overcome language problems on both sides.

DEVELOPING SKILLS

Japanese and North American managers who work and meet with each other should attend meeting leadership training together for two very good reasons:

1. Both North Americans and Japanese will benefit from honed skills. In spite of what they think, most North Americans need to improve their meeting leadership skills significantly.

2. When meeting leaders and participants learn the same procedural steps and process skills, they have more realistic expectations of the course of meetings and meeting members are able to help the leader through problem areas or misunderstandings. For example, any member can summarize, ask for the opinion of a quiet participant, or check for understanding. The result is shared leadership and shared responsibility for a meeting's success.

One simple, yet effective, method for helping everyone remember the critical steps is to post them on a wall chart on conference room walls. Wall charts offer a quick summary—and a constant reminder—of how meetings should proceed.

The critical steps and process skills of meeting leadership are not difficult to learn, and they result in immediate improvement of the quality and efficiency of meetings. In a very short time, people will be impressed with the noticeable improvements.

8

ROLE CLARITY:

A Day-to-Day Struggle to Keep

Things Straight

*They will not allow us to say "report to." They don't understand
why it's important for us to know who we report to. They've got
lifetime employment . . . so they don't have to worry about who
they work for. . . .*

AMERICAN MANAGER

As JAPANESE OPERATIONS get started in North America, relationships
between Japanese and local employees often lack clearly defined
roles. Japanese employees might seem confident (or at least uncon-
cerned) about their roles in the organization, but to North Americans,
the boundaries, responsibilities, and obligations of individuals in
Japanese organizations can be uncomfortably vague. A majority of
North Americans report that this ambiguity is causing them to be less
effective than they could be.

Role clarity is important to North Americans because of what their
past experience has taught them. Many come from companies where

organizational structures changed frequently, requiring the establishment of new job functions and reporting relationships. North Americans have learned to cope with this changing environment by working out written agreements with their superiors regarding job responsibilities and performance expectations. Managers and employees often are hired to do very specific things, and role clarity gives employees a sense of purpose and direction.

Read between the lines in the lists of problems or grievances in Chapter 5 of this book. As you'll recall, the lists were drafted during one of the periodic "crisis" retreats of American and Japanese managers at a four-year-old Japanese manufacturing facility in the Midwest. The problems that were frustrating each side were revealed in a heartfelt and emotional manner. Both sides agreed to work on resolving their differences and felt progress could be made.

But viewed from the perspective of role clarity, the gulf between the two sides seems vast. The American managers plead for open and honest information sharing, recognition, a sense of involvement, consistency in the way they are treated, direct and unambiguous communication, and clearly stated expectations. All of their concerns are focused on making their individual roles explicit and understandable.

Now look at the primary concerns of the Japanese managers: total commitment, sharing the burdens of the situation, working together as a team, accepting overlaps and duplication in duties and responsibilities. The message is just the opposite: Please stop being so concerned about yourselves and your individual roles. In the overall scheme of things, they just aren't that important.

Significantly, after nearly four years of working together, both sides have reached opposite conclusions about why the morale of local employees seems to be plummeting. The Americans, frustrated and angry about the continuing vagueness of roles, have begun to question the very purpose of their employment: Are we just "playing roles like actors in a play," they wonder; are we hired to make it *look* like local managers are involved in an operation that is really run by the Japanese? Or are we meant to be fully functional members of the management team? Role confusion—due in part to unclear job descriptions, the ambiguity of the decision-making process, and an inability to understand how the system works—has led to a feeling of helplessness among the Americans, of being unable to use their talents and abilities, of having no way to advance within the company.

TRANSPARENCY

Role clarity relates to what an increasing number of North American and Japanese observers call the *transparency* of the Japanese organization. For a Japanese organization to be transplanted successfully, many believe it must be transparent enough to allow individuals to see through it and understand how things work. That understanding should include the roles of individuals, the rules that govern their relationships with one another, and the way decisions are made. How transparent do North Americans find Japanese organizations? "It's about as clear as mud," says one American manager. "You have a hard time figuring out what your role is and a hard time figuring out the roles of the Japanese you work with. Supposedly, these special relationships between us and the Japanese are going to evolve over time, but sometimes it seems like we're all just getting more confused."

His response is typical. Indeed, the problem is starting to worry many Japanese executives. Keizai Doyukai, head of the Japan Association of Corporate Executives, has warned that the lack of management transparency might make it difficult to attract foreign employees. Ultimately, the problem could impede overseas expansion. What are some of the reasons for the confusion, and is it such a bad thing?*

STRUCTURAL DIFFERENCES

The typical North American organization is a pyramid composed of blocks, each block representing a clearly defined job (Figure 8.1). There is little space between the blocks. The structure is rigid. A reporting system with a clear chain of command keeps it intact. Managers on one level evaluate those below them on how well they achieve their objectives and discharge the duties listed on job descriptions.

* *Automotive News*, May 28, 1990, p. 6.

FIGURE 8.1
**DIFFERENCES IN HOW JAPANESE AND NORTH AMERICAN
ORGANIZATIONS FUNCTION**

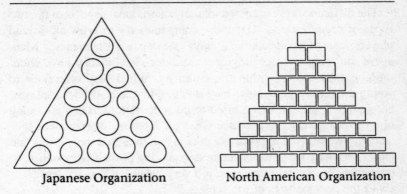

Japanese Organization   North American Organization

Note: In the Japanese organization, there may be a lot of space between jobs.
       In the North American organization, there is little space between jobs.

In the typical Japanese organization, the structure is often described as far more fluid. Instead of blocks, jobs are better described as circles with varying amounts of space between them. The spaces between jobs make mutual cooperation in the form of consensus decision making and *nemawashi* essential. Otherwise, employees would not understand what was expected of them. In contrast, the North American organization spends much effort on minimizing the space between jobs; without a clear understanding of where jobs begin and end, the structure might weaken and even collapse. But in the Japanese organization, spaces between jobs—far from being a liability—give the organization flexibility.

Employees can circulate freely throughout the organization without becoming confused or disoriented. They learn more about the company with each new assignment. Eventually they understand how to harmonize their own individual contributions with the organization's goals and focus. Unlike the North American organization, peer-to-peer relationships are often more important than relationships between levels because relationships, not reporting arrangements, give the organization its strength. Thus, while North Americans might be evaluated by superiors on whether their performance meets well-defined criteria, employees in a Japanese organization might be evaluated on how well they get along with others. "If peers get along well, this is a positive reflection on the manager," notes a Japanese consultant. "Japanese companies don't emphasize performance, but rather how well subordinates work with peers."

The differences are reflected in many operational aspects of the two types of organizations. "Japanese companies try to grow all-around players instead of specialists," says one Japanese manager. "Managers can make correct judgments and decisions if they have wide-ranging experiences within the company. When they offer jobs to young university graduates, they don't show them job descriptions, because they are not being hired to do specific jobs. They are being hired to accumulate experience." Says a Japanese employment specialist, "We find the appropriate person and then find the appropriate job. That's why we have a good understanding of their personality. In the United States, you make the job very clear, but you are less clear about the personalities of job seekers."

In actual practice, the differences between North American and Japanese organizations are not as clear-cut as we have portrayed them. Japanese organizations have a stronger vertical relationship (albeit masked) and many North American organizations are far less rigid than we have described. In fact, progressive North American organizations are rapidly moving toward looser, more flexible structures.

Jack Welch, CEO of General Electric, calls the idea the "boundaryless company . . . where we knock down the walls that separate us from one another on the inside and from our key constituencies on the outside."* The goal is to get ideas through the organization to completion faster by using empowered, cross-functional, or other teams. Because individuals participate on several teams, they play many roles—leader, representative of their department, representative of a technological discipline, doer, and so forth. Similar to Japanese companies' attempts to bring more flexible organization structures into the United States, Canada, and Mexico, North American attempts at boundaryless organizations have met with mixed results. They are all running into managerial expectations shaped by models from the past that are incongruent with present organizational needs. The difference is that North American organizations are acutely aware of the problems and are actively trying to correct them.

* *1990 General Electric Annual Report.*

Coordinators

Organization charts of many new Japanese operations in North America would show one Japanese at the top of the organization and other Japanese in staff positions, such as Finance. North Americans would fill all other positions. Often not shown are the Japanese "shadows" (called coordinators or advisors), who are paired with many North American managers and supervisors. These coordinators are meant to be on-the-spot trainers and mentors to the North American managers as they learn the company's practices and values. In theory, the Japanese coordinator is not supposed to have decision-making authority. His purpose is not to manage but to develop local managers. The local manager has the authority, is the key decision maker, and has the title. The Japanese coordinator is meant to be all but invisible in the decision-making process.

The coordinator system has proved tremendously effective in many Japanese organizations in North America. The coordinator brings with him knowledge of the larger organization, its mission and values, as well as specific technical knowledge of machinery, systems, and procedures. American managers soon learn their coordinators' value in terms of technical expertise and in checking decisions of all types. In theory, coordinators are not able to veto decisions made by local managers, but because of their ability to communicate directly with higher management in Japanese, their suggestions are usually given considerable weight.

The Japanese coordinator system must be given a great deal of credit for the initial success of most start-ups of Japanese companies in North America. Many companies have reached target production levels far earlier than expected, with far fewer problems. More important, the coordinator system has been the primary method of establishing the organization's vision and values. The coordinators communicate the organization's vision and values through their actions and continually reinforce their importance.

While the benefits of coordinators are many, their presence for long periods of time also causes problems. At one Japanese operation in the northeastern United States, a few vague statements were included in its mission statement about working as a team and partnerships, but the details that would define actual methods of working together were never articulated. In fairness, this Japanese company has demonstrated a commitment to local control elsewhere and has been successful in giving local supervisors and managers considerable autonomy. But it's not happening here. "One of our biggest problems is our Japanese coordinators telling our supervisors how to manage personnel-related problems, which is not what they're supposed to be doing," says the American human resources manager.

> They're supposed to provide technical advice and assistance, but they naturally have their opinions on personnel, promotions, job rotation, and so on. They're not supposed to dictate those decisions, but they try. In fact, they have a tendency to run over our American supervisors.
>
> Somehow our first-line [American] supervisors and managers have to say, "I appreciate your opinion, but I think this is the best way to do it." But we can't get them to use their authority. Why don't the Americans assert themselves? They feel like the Japanese must know more than they do. They feel that asserting themselves might jeopardize their jobs since so many Japanese make it clear you've got to do it their way. They feel caught in a no-win situation.
>
> Trying to define roles and responsibilities is a constant frustration. But we're never going to be able to get our local managers to grow up— that's the term we use—until we can do that. When supervisors ask, "Who is the boss?" our answer has always been, "You are," but in reality the Japanese coordinators insist on wielding authority. It's essential that we make our supervisors understand that the Japanese coordinator is eventually going to return to Japan, while they're going to be stuck here with the consequences of decisions. But if they can't learn to make decisions, we've got problems.

This has been going on for *six* years. Not only is the company making no headway on the problem of developing and empowering American supervisors but role-clarity problems flare up with every new batch of coordinators from Japan. The dilemma of being expected to make decisions without the power to do so proves too much for some supervisors. Many have asked to return to nonsupervisory positions. "They can't handle the stress. They're getting hit from all sides—from their production associates, from the Japanese, from us."

At one Japanese operation in the South, group leaders (supervisors) have a North American manager, a Japanese manager, *and* a Japanese coordinator. "They usually don't contradict each other," says the American human resources manager, "but each will have enough different suggestions and comments that cause the group leader a great deal of uncertainty about exactly how his superiors expect things to get done. It makes it hard to internalize the company's way of doing things, since to the group leader, the company doesn't seem to understand it itself."

As for North American managers, the confusion over responsibilities makes traditional management functions, such as delegation and control, difficult to perform. Says one American manager, "I try to challenge people and give them responsibility. The importance of that is something I've learned to appreciate from the Japanese. Trouble is, I can get people to do things, but I never know if they will be told later to do it differently."

A Japanese coordinator in the Midwest admits, "It can be very hard for American managers to understand that we are *not* their competitors. Most coordinators don't feel the need to throw their weight around. We are not vying with an American manager for the same job." Meanwhile, to the Japanese, the groping for role clarity among North Americans can come across as an obsession with petty concerns, such as personal authority and rank.

Many times the coordinator-manager relationship produces benefits for both the organization and individuals. Four factors usually are present in these situations:

1. The two individuals have a good personal relationship. They respect and like each other. Each has come into the relationship with an open mind about the situation and has been willing to work hard to adapt to it.

2. The coordinator is skillful and sensitive in presenting suggestions. This might result from natural skills or, more often, from skills developed through training (see Chapter 17).

3. The coordinator acts as a two-way communicator. A major function of coordinators often is to act as the "eyes and ears" of management in Japan. They seek a great deal of information from their assigned manager about the manager's function and the organization's overall activities. Unfortunately, many coordinators are more interested in collecting information than sharing it. "You get little pieces of information on a sort of 'this is what you need to know'

basis," says one North American manager. "But you need the bigger picture on company plans and policies. You know the coordinator knows what is coming six months from now, but when they act like it is none of your business, it makes you wonder why the company thinks you took the job—to be a permanent trainee?"

4. The date on which the coordinator position will be eliminated is defined—or there is an understanding that the coordinator position is permanent. North American managers are more than willing to learn from and work with one coordinator for a three-year assignment, and even with a second coordinator for another three years, but it really starts to cause problems when the third coordinator shows up. When the new Japanese coordinator starts the learning cycle at the beginning, North American managers are likely to conclude that all their efforts and achievements to date were wasted. "All the Americans here have changed in some pretty remarkable ways over the past years," says an American in Ohio. "But you would never know it by some of the new Japanese assigned here. They tend to treat you like new hires, like it wasn't your company at all, and as if you've made no contribution to the company's success."

Sometimes, out of necessity, elimination dates for the coordinator position will be pushed back. Coordinators might have to be reinstated if organizational problems arise, but these should be exceptions and seen as such by everyone in the organization. If the coordinator's job is going to be permanent, a title other than coordinator should be used and the position clearly shown on the organization chart.

Japanese coordinators and advisors paired with North American managers don't have an easy time of it either. Told to defer to North Americans in some areas and to take charge in others, the Japanese manager finds the situation even more ambiguous than he's used to in Japan.

In the day-to-day crush of any business operation, especially in the superheated atmosphere of a start-up operation, it can be hard for a Japanese manager to look at all the minor and major interactions that occur daily and stop each time to think, "Is this something more appropriately dealt with by the American manager hired for this purpose, or is this something that I can intervene in directly? Will my action contribute to the blending of local and Japanese talents here, or will it confuse and antagonize people?" The dilemma can make

Japanese managers seem inconsistent. It leads to widely shared complaints: "The Japanese just can't make decisions," or "You never know what the Japanese are going to do."

Who's in Charge

Japanese organizations in North America often are quite creative when it comes to titles. They feel that this is one way of meeting the needs of North Americans. However, some North Americans suspect that this is partly to confuse people about who is in charge. Whether this is true or not, confusion does arise, particularly when the North American titles don't fit clearly in the Japanese hierarchy. One senior manager of a financial firm describes the situation this way:

> Often, companies create a complete range of fancy titles that appear to confer some power to the local staff but are, in fact, window dressing only. Unless one has a title that has a direct equivalent in the Japanese system, e.g., Managing Director (*Bucho*), then one knows that one is being shunted into *Gaijin* Land, rather than Japan Land.

Role confusion also can result from the perceived "weak" leadership of Japanese presidents or general managers. It's an uninformed characterization in many ways, but it does illustrate differences between how North Americans and Japanese view leadership and the confusion Japanese managers create when they fail to clarify the reasons for their actions or policies.

As we've suggested, North Americans might not understand the rationale for leadership that employs few outward signs of control or direction. They even equate it with powerlessness and impotence. "No one is in charge" is a complaint often heard among North Americans in Japanese companies. Someone is in charge, of course, but that someone is often thousands of miles away and is unknown to the North Americans.

Japanese companies like to control overseas operations closely, and many Japanese managers admit that Tokyo gives them little freedom to act autonomously. The business day ends in North America while it is just beginning in Japan, so there is plenty of opportunity for a steady stream of evening faxes and telephone calls. Major and minor policy decisions often are made at headquarters. That might make perfect sense, especially during a start-up phase. However, it comes at the expense of the unending frustration of many North American managers, who frequently see their decisions nullified or reversed in a mysterious communication from Tokyo. It is not pleasant for local Japanese managers, either, to have to somehow forge a consensus around a decision they might have had no role in reaching.

The more Americans feel excluded from an active role and the more confused they are about how decisions are being made, the more ineffectual Japanese presidents or general managers seem. "We really need a boss, not someone who just serves as a conduit for dictates from Tokyo," says an American manager. This observation is made frequently. "You feel twice removed from what's really going on," says another manager. "If you don't know who is making decisions, you can't appeal to them or even understand them." Typically, in a North American organization, when top managers are indecisive, middle managers feel more freedom to act on their own. That rarely happens among North Americans in Japanese organizations.

Another consequence of the mystery of senior leadership in Japanese organizations is a perception among North American managers that someone with an arbitrary title and unclear place on the organization chart is really calling the shots—a chief of staff or executive coordinator, for instance, whose agenda and authority are unknown. North Americans often view this mysterious figure with a great deal of mistrust. Further, they might develop a sense that the Japanese are divided into factions, all jockeying for some position or authority that the North Americans can't comprehend. The constant stream of visiting "fire fighters" at some Japanese operations also adds to the confusion. Who are they? What fires were they sent to put out? Answers are seldom forthcoming.

Imposing Role Clarity

Methods for creating role clarity are tightly entwined with the performance management issues discussed in Chapter 11. The concepts of setting key result areas and performance objectives, both essential elements of performance management, are methods North American managers use to establish role clarity. Systems can be developed to mesh individual needs for role clarity with organizational realities of looser, more flexible organizations.

But who is responsible for role clarity? Since Japanese and North American notions of performance management can be so different, some local managers observe that you can wait indefinitely for Japanese organizations to delineate clear managerial roles. These North Americans believe the reason is the unfamiliarity of Japanese managers with the need of local employees for clear role objectives and performance feedback. It's beyond their experience. Overlapping and ambiguous boundaries, task duplication, collegial leadership, and more are all part of a Japanese system that works well without clear boundaries and individual performance parameters. "They've absolutely made an art of the lack of role clarity," suggests one North American manager:

> Everyone's nose is always in everyone else's business. It encourages people to test the limits of their jobs, to be willing to do anything, to expand into other people's jobs, to overlap with others while others overlap with them. It's why their suggestion systems work so well. It's why people are always looking for ways to improve someone's job. It's where they get their productivity and commitment. They really have no choice but to be concerned about the whole company, since they don't get little pieces of it to wrap themselves up in.

North Americans *can* learn to live with a lack of role clarity. In fact, there are advantages to looser systems: They allow quicker response to organizational needs and provide more opportunity for job expansion and enrichment. The problem is that most North Americans don't see the advantages. They only see the disadvantages. In many Japanese organizations, no one has tried to communicate the advantages. Such efforts might well be part of an orientation program for new North American employees.

The task of establishing some form of role clarity might fall more to the North Americans in Japanese organizations than to the Japanese themselves. This, in fact, might be one area in which North Americans can make a clear contribution to creating the "blended" organization. "Part of our process of maturing in a Japanese company is forcing a certain amount of role clarity on our Japanese colleagues," says an American manager, who offers this advice to other Americans:

> Go in to the boss and say, "I believe these are my responsibilities at this point in time. This is what I intend to do; here's how I intend to measure

my performance; and here are the five goals I've set. Let's go over them one by one. And let's make sure we agree. Then you will sign this summary that indicates that we both agree on what I am supposed to accomplish. In six months, you and I will evaluate my performance on those areas we've identified as most important. And then at the end of the year, I'll schedule a performance appraisal with you. I'll send you all my data in advance."

Such actions would make many North Americans uncomfortable, and it would "shock the pants off the Japanese," adds the American. "But just you wait. It's going to start happening more and more."

Another approach that Japanese managers might be more comfortable with involves setting up a joint committee of Japanese and North Americans to clarify and define job responsibilities and establish individual key result areas (Chapter 11). North American managers could take the lead in setting up and directing such meetings. The result would be a document that would serve as a basis for a goal-setting discussion between a North American manager and his or her Japanese boss. Such role-clarity committees are a common device in the United States and Canada because they expose unplanned overlaps or holes in the coverage of responsibilities.

9

KEY PRINCIPLES OF HUMAN INTERACTION:

WHAT EFFECTIVE LEADERS IN NORTH AMERICA MUST DO

Many would argue that a distinctly American impulse is to put the best face on things, to be upbeat and cheerful, to appear in control and successful even when uncertainty is high and the future looks bleak. The Japanese, it appears, bias their assessments in the opposite direction. From the Japanese mother who turns aside praise of her child's piano playing with "mada heta desu!" ("no, it is still bad!"), to the Japanese politicians who, despite Japan's booming economy, persist in protesting the country's weak and dependent posture in world affairs—the Japanese seem to color their evaluations of nearly everything with a large dose of pessimism, humility, and understatement.

AMERICAN RESEARCHER EXPLAINING
WHY HIS STUDIES SHOWING LOW JOB
SATISFACTION IN JAPAN MAY REFLECT
A "RESTLESS STRIVING FOR PERFECTION"*

* Lincoln, J. R. "Employee Work Attitudes and Management Practices in the U.S. and Japan: Evidence from a Large Comparative Survey." *California Management Review,* Vol. 32(1), Fall 1989, p. 92.

*Americans don't seem to understand that everything we do
we do because our very survival is at stake . . . that every
minute of every day should reflect that struggle.*

JAPANESE MANAGER AT A U.S. DIVISION
OF ONE OF JAPAN'S LARGEST
AUTOMOBILE MANUFACTURERS

SUCCESSFUL NORTH AMERICAN leaders do certain things very well
during daily interactions with colleagues and subordinates. A lucky
few seem to exercise these skills intuitively. Often they are labeled
"natural leaders." But for most effective leaders, the skills that contribute to their success had to be learned and diligently practiced.

Effective leadership behaviors have been described and cataloged
in numerous ways. Our research has led us to group them into four key
principles,* which are an integral part of a training program completed by more than three million American supervisors and managers in many of America's most successful companies. Three key
principles used by successful leaders in daily interactions with others
are explained below, and the fourth principle is covered in Chapter 10.

These key principles help managers become effective teachers,
coaches, motivators, and organizers in a North American setting.
Japanese managers seem to handle several of these key principles very
well, especially seeking and developing ideas. In other areas, specifically in the critical area of handling the self-esteem of North Americans, Japanese managers appear to have much to learn.

KEY PRINCIPLE 1: MAINTAIN OR ENHANCE
SELF-ESTEEM

In a North American workplace, the importance of self-esteem—the
quality of feeling good about one's self and job—cannot be overesti-

---

* These four key principles are part of Development Dimensions International's
Techniques for an Empowered Workforceᔆᴹ training program. Copyright © 1990
by Development Dimensions International, Inc. World rights reserved.

mated. When self-esteem is high, morale usually is, too. Productivity is increased when people are committed to doing their best. If self-esteem is low, employees will not make the extra effort required for *kaizen* or take the chances required to develop creative ideas. They will withdraw within themselves.

Japanese managers easily acknowledge the importance of self-esteem in Japanese and North American cultures, but actually practicing behavior designed to maintain or enhance self-esteem proves troublesome for many. Their reactions in training programs (conducted in Japanese) that teach how to maintain or enhance self-esteem suggest that what North American managers might consider worthwhile efforts to enhance self-esteem is to Japanese managers an example of unnecessary and illogical flattery. They see such efforts as a violation of the "rules" governing superior/subordinate relationships—one rule being that Japanese employees neither expect nor desire praise.

"Pride is not a thing desired in subordinates," says one Japanese executive. "Managers feel that self-esteem and pride are the same thing, and are reluctant to maintain self-esteem lest they increase pride." Another agrees: "Sometimes managers think that praise makes the other person swell-headed, which is not desirable. Because the workplace is a place of continuous training, being satisfied with one's own achievements is not good for employees."

According to some Japanese managers, Japanese culture itself, with its emphasis on modesty and getting along with others, poses built-in barriers to effectively using self-esteem boosters to increase job performance. "Japanese people probably have more pride than any other race," says one manager, "but we are conditioned to be careful about expressing self-esteem. It might be taken as boasting by others, and boasting is one of the most displeasing behaviors in Japanese society. There is simply no place in Japanese society to openly express, discuss, or talk about personal self-esteem. Therefore, we are very awkward in praising and enhancing someone's self-esteem."

One result is that when Japanese managers do praise Japanese subordinates, subordinates often think they are joking. "An employee who is praised unexpectedly by a manager would feel uneasy," says one Japanese manager. "He would wonder about the manager's intention. Instead of feeling good about the praise, the employee would probably think the manager was being ironic and that he was using that irony to criticize the employee's performance." Genuine praise in the Japanese workplace, this manager says, can be very modest and fleeting. "The employee will catch the manager's satisfaction, but the words he uses will be too subtle for non-Japanese employees."

Expectations are very different in North America. An American production manager at a Japanese auto parts manufacturer in the Midwest describes in dramatic fashion what happens when these expectations clash with reality in Japanese operations:

> We recently had a quality audit by our largest customer. Our rating was far higher than we had expected. It was even higher than levels in Japan. We were thrilled. It was the big payoff for all the hard work we had done. But, of course, our [Japanese] director of quality gets up in front of all the managers and says, "In regard to the recent quality rating, the current rating is 4.5. The new goal is 5.0." That was it. Not a word of praise. Not a sign of emotion. You could feel the mood drop to the floor in the room. Some people were almost in tears.

The principle of maintaining or enhancing self-esteem can be difficult for North American managers as well. One problem North American and Japanese managers face is understanding the need to be specific in reinforcement—that is, giving an explicit example of what was done correctly or well. Nonspecific or vague words of praise can come off as insincere—just as Japanese managers suspect—and can even damage self-esteem if it causes employees to conclude that someone is trying to manipulate them with praise. Japanese managers in training sessions generally find that the best way to overcome their reluctance to praise others is to be very specific. They feel more at ease saying, "You did an excellent job of having the XYZ machine retooled in a twenty-four-hour period," than "You are doing a good job."

Still, it can be very difficult for Japanese managers to adjust to the need to practice behavior that maintains and enhances the self-esteem of North Americans—or even to perceive the need. For example, one Japanese manager in California explains that his experience as a section chief for a financial services company in Tokyo did little to prepare him for the reality of working with North Americans:

> We focus on pointing out mistakes; to Americans, that makes us seem negative all the time, although we are only trying to get people to look at problems logically and thoroughly. We can't understand the use of praise in America. It seems childish and superficial, but everyone

seems to need it. A nurse recently told me, "Super job!" during a company physical when I gave her my urine sample. She seemed to think I needed "positive feedback" for peeing into a bottle. It's very hard, especially when communication is difficult, to react to all the psychological requirements of Americans—to understand their need for reassurance and support and being pointed in a direction that will further their careers.

Another problem Japanese managers seem to have in dealing with the self-esteem of North American employees is a tendency to focus on the person instead of the situation. The difference, for example, is saying, "Let's look at what happened and try to figure out what went wrong," instead of "You screwed up and really made a mess of it!" By focusing on the problem, the individual's self-esteem is maintained, and he or she is motivated to find a solution. If the individual is blamed, he or she will become defensive and might blame others for the problem.

Whatever effect placing blame has in Japan, cultural differences in how it is perceived in North America means that it serves no constructive purpose. Indeed, the resistance and embarrassment caused by blaming employees will likely *degrade* performance instead of improve it. A Japanese production manager in California discusses one lesson he's learned after two years in America:

Here, when people have problems or make mistakes, it's supposed to be discussed calmly and in an "upbeat" way. You almost have to negotiate with people to get them to change. Japanese managers might not want to spend a lot of time with this. To them, it could be enough to say, "Here is your error. Here is how to correct it. Now do it, please." What else is required?

But in America, such actions can be seen as blaming individuals in front of others, which is very embarrassing to Americans, but far less so to Japanese, because we are used to sitting in one big room and always know when a manager points out something wrong to a subordinate. Sometimes when a Japanese manager speaks roughly with a subordinate, there is even a feeling, "Well, it's just his turn to get it. Next time it's mine." Many Japanese even view this as positive. It indicates that a manager has expectations of you and is willing to teach you by pointing out the flaws in your performance. But if you are not careful in America, the same behavior can make you seem unreasonable, like you enjoy picking on people.

The differences in perceptions of criticism and blame among Japanese and North Americans can be striking. Many North Americans have experienced scenes like the one described below by an American manager in the Midwest. Before the Japanese president described here was reassigned, his behavior had caused him to be widely detested by the American work force. His style of leading resulted in growing morale and productivity problems. Even by Japanese standards, his tenure was short:

> When a group of team and area leaders came back from four weeks of training in Japan, there was a reception at the plant. The [Japanese] president gets up to make a few remarks to welcome them back. What does he say? He chews out both the Americans and their Japanese trainers for "childish behavior" and "lack of seriousness" because he had heard a few stories about a couple of loud parties they had in Japan. He really blasted them. The Americans were stunned. Some of them walked out. The strange thing is that the Japanese trainers sat there digging the whole thing. They thought it was a "pep talk" about not letting up and remaining fully committed to the venture. To them, this was how a leader was supposed to behave.

The Japanese president's behavior shows how behavior that is acceptable in Japan can backfire in North America. One Japanese consultant says that older managers in Japan still tend to feel that, "The rod makes people stronger. Scolding people in front of others is good. Older managers feel, 'If I'm impressed with you, I will be very hard on you. This will continue your development.' " While younger Japanese employees might be losing patience with this type of stern, scolding manager, the consultant says, the behavior is still common. This comes as a big surprise to North Americans. An American employee with a Japanese electronics manufacturer in Tokyo told *Ashai News* that the first time he made a mistake on the job, his *"kacho"* yelled at him in front of others, "How stupid you are!" "I was shocked and depressed," the American recalled. "Then he yelled the same thing at a Japanese employee, who didn't seem to care much at all and continued doing his job."

The American's shocked reaction shows how this behavior runs counter to the basic leadership principles of North American business, especially the principle of maintaining or enhancing self-esteem. "To the Japanese, the ideal floor supervisor is a stern disciplinarian who is not afraid to go berserk sometimes," says an American manager in New England who has spent a decade working for several Japanese employers. "The Japanese like to say that what we need here is an assistant manager with horns. That means one needs a balance: a soft manager and a hard assistant manager. Unfortunately, with our work force, the manager with horns is virtually always a lousy manager."

In addition to public blaming, Japanese managers also might display what, for North Americans, is a degree of emotionalism that seems strangely out of place in the North American workplace. North Americans usually attribute it to the immense pressure Japanese managers are under to succeed. Expectations and performance targets often are very high. Performance in overseas assignments can make or break careers. Failure simply is not an option. "The wire snaps much quicker," says an American manager, describing the behavior of a Japanese production manager who has since been reassigned:

> His style of management, if you can call it that, included dropping in/out baskets on the floor and kicking them across the room, emptying wastebaskets on people's desks, walking into a room, yelling, "All of you should pack your bags and go," and drilling a finger into your chest as he spoke, his face inches from yours. When I complained about his style to other Japanese advisors, they said, "That's nothing. You should see him in Japan."
>
> His behavior is understandable in a lot of ways. Imagine yourself having to deal with a foreign language day in and day out, with people you probably don't understand very well. Meantime, the company is putting pressure on you to produce, produce, produce, while cutting costs all the time. How would you react? Who could be "lovable" all the time under those circumstances?

Related to this emotionalism is a phenomenon that might be termed "management by guilt" or "psychological blackmail," as one North American manager puts it. For instance, in a role-playing exercise conducted with Japanese managers during a training program, the first response to the chronic lateness of a hypothetical subordinate was anger and a desire to instill a deep sense of guilt and even shame in the subordinate. In role-playing situations, the tardy subordinate was told that she was embarrassing the supervisor, herself, and even the company by coming in late. "How can you persist in doing such a thing?"

the managers asked. "How can you let the group down?" These managers needed to learn the resentment such an approach would cause in North America. The more effective response would have involved exploring the cause of her lateness, offering to help, and gaining her commitment to action—while maintaining the self-esteem of the subordinate relative to the parts of her job she does well.

Chronic lateness, it should be pointed out, is a problem managers rarely encounter in Japan, and not surprisingly, few Japanese managers seem to know how to deal with it. It will be encountered in North America, however, as will other problems that are virtually nonexistent in Japan. That makes it important for Japanese managers to learn local approaches in dealing with local problems. "Japanese managers sometimes purposefully hurt a subordinate's self-esteem to activate the individual," a Japanese manager in the United States points out. "The purpose is to get him mad and thus to work harder." But the effects can be completely different in the United States, this manager acknowledges, where instead of increasing motivation, it can do just the opposite.

KEY PRINCIPLE 2: LISTEN AND RESPOND WITH EMPATHY

North Americans want their superiors and colleagues to pay attention to what they are saying and to be responsive to what they are feeling. This gives Japanese managers in North American organizations a double challenge. First, they must truly understand what the individual is trying to communicate and the feelings or emotions behind that communication. Second, they must communicate that understanding back to the individual. That's empathy. (Without the second part, the first part is largely unimportant.)

Here are two examples of typical situations faced by American managers and suggested empathetic replies:

1. **Situation One:** It's a typical summer week in the shipping department. Almost everyone is on vacation, including your boss, the plant manager. Your boss's phone rings and you take the call. It's the manager of the customer service department with a complaint about an order shipped last week. She's very angry and starts the conversa-

tion by saying, "When are you people going to get your act together down there?"

Empathetic Reply: "I can understand why you're angry. I'd certainly be angry if I thought customer orders weren't being filled promptly and accurately. If you can provide me with all the details, I'll check into the situation immediately and follow up with you when I find out what happened."

2. **Situation Two:** You are the parts manager of an automobile plant. Last week, Bob, one of your best supervisors, placed a rush order with a distributor. Bob has just received a call from them, alerting him that additional parts not ordered were included with the shipment. This means that Bob will need to double-check the entire shipment for these parts and make arrangements to return them. He is in your office now and is very upset. "Do you know how far behind this is going to put the plant's production schedule? This isn't our error; why do *we* have to check it?"

Empathetic Reply: "I know it will take a long time to check the shipment, Bob. Because it's the distributor's error, I can understand why you're so angry. I'd be angry, too. Now let's talk about what we can do."

It is important to distinguish empathy from sympathy. North American managers working in Japanese organizations report that their Japanese managers can be extremely *sympathetic* when an individual faces a family crisis or other situation that needs immediate attention. But communication and cultural barriers seem to make them less able to appear empathetic to North Americans, which is a deficit that may limit their effectiveness with North Americans.

The perceived lack of empathy often is caused by the difficulty Japanese managers have appreciating the sometimes bewildering variety of social, economic, and family challenges that local employees face. As the example of the chronically late employee (in the role-playing exercise mentioned previously) indicates, Japanese managers might react with disbelief and even anger to common occurrences in the North American workplace. "My Japanese colleagues can't seem to understand when outside events take precedence over work," says an American manager working for a Japanese firm in Canada. "My son was in the finals of a hockey tournament, and I felt guilty leaving work to go to another town to see him play. No one, in any way, indicated that they understood my situation. In many ways, they indicated disapproval."

Moreover, many Japanese managers say that empathy doesn't play much of a role in the Japanese workplace, where hierarchical rules more closely circumscribe the interactions between superiors and subordinates. "Japanese find it easy to be sympathetic," a Japanese consultant says, "but it can be hard to express empathy, since empathy puts two people on the same status level, and Japanese are acutely aware of status differences and act accordingly. In the United States, subordinates might feel equal with the boss and expect to be treated as such. In Japan, subordinates do not feel equal with the boss."

Empathy might be similar to *omoiyari* (ō-mō-ē-yă-rē), the Japanese term for the consideration of others and their feelings, which is an exquisitely developed aspect of Japanese culture. The difference is that this feeling is often expressed in dozens of subtle and, sometimes, nonverbal ways in Japan, whereas empathy in a Western sense requires "talking through" with another person what that person is feeling. As one Japanese manager points out, "When your English is inadequate, it is very hard to respond empathetically." It is also hard to gauge the level of empathy that situations require in North America, this manager says. "Because Japanese managers are so sensitive to saying and doing the right things, they might refrain from expressing even necessary empathetic words because they are unsure of their appropriateness."

North Americans, however, might take little of this into consideration, and instead view a lack of expressed empathy comments as a lack of understanding and concern. Japanese managers who have developed an ability to listen and respond with empathy have learned it is a key skill in recognizing and promoting cultural understanding and appreciation. They understand that just as the Japanese expect North Americans to take their backgrounds into consideration and to be appreciative of "where they are coming from," North Americans expect the same from their Japanese colleagues.

But the Japanese must guard against stereotyping. North Americans don't want to be treated exclusively as blacks, whites, Hispanics, Native Americans, men, or women. They want to be treated as individuals. Empathy must be relative to an individual. Although individuals might be affected by cultural or gender differences, it is the individual who counts.

Fortunately, in training Japanese managers to use Key Principle 2, we find that they have little difficulty in understanding the different expectations of North American workers and in learning how to respond with empathy. Once the language barrier is broken, they have tremendous insights into situations and have no trouble expressing sincere feelings to the individual. Language and training are the keys.

KEY PRINCIPLE 3: ASK FOR HELP AND ENCOURAGE INVOLVEMENT

North Americans want their superiors to seek their input, ask for their help, encourage their involvement in solving problems, and make them feel that their ideas are important and that they make a meaningful contribution. This third key principle is often a strength for Japanese managers, who are used to pulling together the ideas of many in the decision-making process. But while seeking ideas, asking for help, and encouraging involvement are strengths, some Japanese run the risk of seeking too much information. To North Americans, Japanese managers can seem to have an endless appetite for quantitative data. "They want everything quantified. Even things that can't possibly be projected," says one American manager. "They take quantitative analysis to the extreme," agrees another manager.

Some observers speculate that the Japanese fascination with numbers reflects their lack of confidence in the use of the English language and in the judgment of American managers. Quantification gives them a universal language (numbers) and more confidence in a North American manager's judgment. Others note that relentless "intelligence gathering" is a common trait of Japanese organizations. Japanese managers are "vacuum cleaners sucking up everything," says an American manager. "You spend most of your time here just answering questions." It also should be noted that many Japanese managers come from environments dominated by a "zero defect" mentality that makes data gathering to investigate the causes of problems—not just the symptoms—a never-ending process. In this area, many North American managers have much to learn.

It is important to remember, however, that seeking data is not the same as asking for help and encouraging involvement. With no real analysis, little "ownership" of the solution is developed. Consistent performance gains tend to come from asking questions that help individuals see what questions need to be answered and then guiding them in obtaining the information they need to reach a solution on their own. Instead, Japanese managers often seem to gather information from North Americans for their own private purposes.

KEYS TO HUMAN INTERACTION

Our experience in training millions of people throughout the world in these three key principles leads us to feel that they are important determiners of success in all human interactions. They are just as important in family interactions as they are at work. When a manager uses the first three key principles, he or she is known as practicing participative management or employee involvement. Effective use of the first three key principles forms a base for the fourth key principle—offer help without removing responsibility for action—which creates feelings of empowerment and is considered in the next chapter.

ARE THE KEY PRINCIPLES MORE OFTEN APPLIED UPWARD THAN DOWNWARD IN JAPAN?

A good Japanese friend of ours argues that it is more important for Japanese employees to learn to use the key principles with their superiors than superiors with their employees. He explains that because of the respect that comes from rank in Japan, it is appropriate for employees to quickly learn how to maintain the self-esteem of the boss by exaggerated praise over his insightful ideas and contributions. An effective subordinate must be sensitive to his boss's feelings even though it might not be appropriate for him to express it. And it is a common ploy of employees to lay out a vast amount of research data in front of a boss, pretend that they have no idea what to do, and then ask for the boss's help in solving the problem.

Thus, our friend says that Japanese managers know from experience how to use the key principles—but they have to learn how to turn them around and use them with their subordinates.

10

EMPOWERMENT

I compare what some American companies are doing with what I see happening at Japanese-run companies and I don't see how Japanese companies are going to keep their competitive edge. Maybe not now, but a few years from now, they are going to start falling behind.

AMERICAN MANAGER

Empowerment, as most of us understand the term, means shared decision making. Power is the part of the word to remember—the power to be responsible, to do things that matter, to take control. If there's anything similar in Japan, it's kaizen, *which is sometimes mistaken by North Americans for empowerment. Kaizen, however, is about giving—your ideas, your energy and commitment, your time—but it's not about taking control. It certainly doesn't mean sharing power. That's why in the end so many Americans become disillusioned by* kaizen. *You give, but you get very little back.*

AMERICAN PRODUCTION
EMPLOYEE

CULTURE AND EMPOWERMENT

JAPANESE EMPLOYEES HAVE long shown a strong personal identification with their jobs and the success of their employers. They see a close relationship among their efforts, the success of the organization, and their future success. If they plan to stay with the organization for all of their working lives, the overlap between self-identity and organization can be nearly complete. The organization encourages this sense of identification with an almost religious set of ceremonies and symbols designed to bond employees to the organization. When you go to work for Mitsubishi, you become a "Mitsubishi man." Your wife is the wife of a Mitsubishi man. If asked to describe you, the first thing neighbors and friends would mention is Mitsubishi. This deep identification of self with the company translates into a work ethic that is a fundamental strength of the Japanese economy.

We've seen how different it can be in North America. In North America, a personal commitment to an employer's values and objectives isn't automatically triggered by organizational membership. There is little in North American society and culture that encourages this commitment, while much works against it. Unlike Japanese employees, most North American employees are culturally conditioned to recognize jobs as legal and contractual relationships more than personal and emotional ones. One American manager, who has worked many years with Japanese and North American employees, says, "Japanese companies expect people to *belong* to the company, whereas the natural tendency of Americans is to think in terms of *working for* the company. This can be one of the most surprising things of all to Japanese managers when they come here. Nothing in their experience has prepared them for people who don't act like they identify completely with the company."

Moreover, it is unlikely North American workers will *ever* identify with their organizations to the same extent as Japanese workers. North Americans rarely feel they are making a lifetime commitment to one company. Their culture tends to separate work from personal life to a much greater extent than does Japanese culture. The primary allegiance of North Americans has traditionally been to themselves, their families, or their professions, instead of to their employers.

Many North American organizations have chipped away at this self-centered orientation and created levels of commitment and identification among local employees every bit as strong as the same levels found among Japanese employees. The key has been empowerment, which in its most basic sense means giving power or decision-making authority to lower organizational levels. Most North American organizations are moving cautiously toward employee empowerment. But many North American organizations have dramatically extended the limits of empowerment by making employees responsible for virtually all of the things once done for them and to them by supervisors and managers (see box below). In these organizations, employees are evaluated according to their achievements, not by how well they follow orders. Because they feel personally responsible for their jobs, they feel they "own" their jobs almost as if they were working for themselves. This sense of ownership and responsibility motivates them to continuously improve their personal productivity, quality, and customer service, because improvements make them feel good about themselves and their roles in the organization. Job success and organizational success become personal success.

EMPOWERMENT

Empowerment occurs when organizational power goes to employees, who then experience a sense of ownership and control over their jobs. An organization empowers its people when it enables employees to take on more authority and responsibility and to make greater use of what they know and can learn.

Specifically, empowerment occurs when the employee:
- Is responsible for designated areas or outputs.
- Has control over resources, systems, methods, and equipment.
- Has control over working conditions and schedules.
- Has authority (within defined limits) to commit the organization.
- Is evaluated by achievements.

ARE JAPANESE COMPANIES EMPOWERING?

To many North Americans, the egalitarian trappings of Japanese organizations and the opportunities they provide for their employees to make decisions about their jobs is truly exciting. This is illustrated by the high morale in many newly opened Japanese facilities. Comments such as these are commonly heard: "They really pay attention to what you say around here." "They don't treat me like a number. They treat me like a person who can think as well as do." New employees love the symbols of the Japanese approach—the lack of reserved parking spaces or special dining rooms for managers; senior managers working in open office areas with everyone else; uniforms that all wear, regardless of rank. One Japanese company gave all new production employees business cards that looked just like those carried by top plant managers. It was a simple gesture, but employees were thrilled and, for months, flashed the cards at the slightest opportunity.

But are Japanese organizations empowering enough? Many Japanese managers looking at current empowerment attempts in North American organizations conclude that Japanese organizations have been doing these things for decades. Empowerment to Japanese managers might appear to be the same as delegating authority and emphasizing teamwork, which is something Japanese organizations feel they do especially well. "What's the fuss?" asks one Japanese manager in the United States. "There are endless examples of empowered teams and groups in Japanese companies. These are part of the Japanese way of doing business."

Is it really? Before we attempt to answer the question, we should look at some of the things we know about empowerment in North America. One way to think about empowerment is to consider it as a continuum, with organizations falling at different places along the continuum. Our research suggests there is nearly a direct, linear relationship between the amount of empowerment individuals feel and the amount of responsibility and authority organizations give to individuals. This relationship is illustrated in Figure 10.1.

The vertical axis shows the amount of empowerment felt. The horizontal axis shows the amount of responsibility and authority given to the employee. At Level 1, the bottom left-hand corner of the figure, individuals have little responsibility and feel little empowerment. Their jobs are designed to eliminate any possibility of making decisions. Their managers are autocratic and dictate precise orders. At Level 7, the other end of the continuum, individuals make many meaningful, job-related decisions themselves, and their superiors respect and trust those decisions. A member of a self-directed work

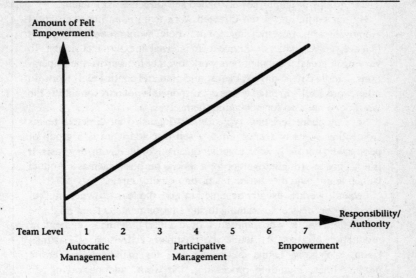

FIGURE 10.1
EMPOWERMENT CONTINUUM

team who has taken on most of the responsibilities listed in Figure 10.2 (see page 114) and who has an empowering supervisor might be at Level 7 on the continuum. A plant manager who is evaluated by results and who has been given latitude of operation also would be at Level 7.

**EMPOWERMENT FROM THE JOB:
THE SELF-DIRECTED WORK TEAM**

The self-directed work team has become an important method of increasing empowerment because of a major obstacle to empowering employees in any organization: Many jobs simply don't provide much leeway for making decisions, taking responsibility, or acting with initiative and independence—three important elements of empowerment. Many jobs in a company might require simple repetitive action, or a job might be paced by a machine. But individuals in such jobs *can*
continued

---

feel empowered if they and others producing a common output work together as a team and make decisions on how the team operates. These groups of employees are called self-directed work teams.

By our definition, a self-directed work team is an intact group of employees who are responsible for a "whole" work process or segment that delivers a product or service to an internal or external customer. To varying degrees, team members work together to improve their operations, handle day-to-day problems, and plan and control their work. In other words, self-directed teams are responsible not only for getting the work done but also for managing themselves.

Several characteristics typically distinguish self-directed teams from other types of teams. First, a self-directed team is a group of people who normally work together on an ongoing, day-to-day basis. It is not a group brought together for a special purpose, such as a product launch team, a quality action team, or a quality circle.

Second, work is usually designed to give the team "ownership" of a product or service. In manufacturing environments, a team might be responsible for a whole product or a clearly defined segment or production process. At Tennessee Eastman, a division of Eastman Kodak Company, teams are responsible for manufacturing entire product lines, including processing, lab work, and packaging. In service environments, self-directed teams usually are responsible for groupings of products or services, often serving clients in a designated geographical area. For example, Aid Association for Lutherans, a large insurance company based in Wisconsin, combined separate life insurance, health insurance, and support service functions into teams that handle all these tasks for clients in a particular region.

Team members have broad job descriptions and share work assignments. Rather than master one narrow job or task, team members are expected, at various times, to perform all the jobs of the team. The most obvious distinguishing characteristics of self-directed teams involve their scope of decision making. Teams are involved in:

- Setting goals and inspecting the team's work (including determining conformance to quality standards)
- Creating schedules and reviewing performance as a group
- Repairing equipment

continued

- Preparing budgets and coordinating the team's work with other departments
- Developing production and work assignment schedules
- Ordering materials, keeping inventories, and dealing with suppliers
- Acquiring training they might need
- Hiring replacements or assuming responsibility for disciplining team members
- Taking responsibility for the quality of products or services

The amount of empowerment created by job structure and leadership style in Japanese organizations in North America is quite different. At the employee level, our observations suggest that most Japanese companies in North America operate at Level 4 or 5 on the empowerment continuum. Initially, this amount of empowerment is very attractive to most North American workers because it is considerably higher than they are accustomed to. The Japanese firm is seen by its new employees as more open to ideas and more trusting of people than typical North American firms. Morale is often very high and employees are enthusiastic about the obvious differences between this new work environment and what they left behind.

Empowerment creates a desire for more empowerment—a lesson that a growing number of North American companies are learning. Consequently, North American companies committed to empowerment also are committed to increasing it as employee skill levels rise. While the ultraempowered organization, the high end of the continuum, is still somewhat experimental in North America, it is clear from our research and the research of others that organizations that dramatically increase their level of employee empowerment to at least Level 6 simultaneously increase employee job satisfaction, productivity, and commitment to continuous improvement.

FIGURE 10.2
INDIVIDUAL OR TEAM JOB RESPONSIBILITIES IN
THREE TYPES OF ORGANIZATIONS

Traditional U.S. Companies	Japanese Companies in North America	Highly Empowered N.A. Companies
Involved in:	Involved in:	Involved in:
Problem solving	Problem solving	Problem solving
Performance of work assignments	Performance of work assignments	Performance of work assignments
	Improving quality and productivity	Improving quality and productivity
	Training each other	Training each other
	Job rotation	Job rotation
	Production goal setting	Production goal setting
	Planning/scheduling work	Planning/scheduling work
	Participation on cross-functional teams	Participation on cross-functional teams
	Who works on what	Who works on what
	Quality audit	Quality audit
	Housekeeping	Housekeeping
	Equipment adjustment, maintenance, repair	Equipment adjustment, maintenance, repair
		Vacation planning
		Absenteeism, tardiness, and performance issues
		Choosing team leader
		Managing suppliers
		Hiring team members
		Direct dealing with internal or external customers
		Purchasing equipment
		Budgeting
		Appraisal of fellow team members
		Compensation

Figure 10.2 shows the empowerment gap between Japanese companies and highly empowered North American companies. The first column shows the responsibilities of individuals in a traditional American company with autocratic leadership. The second column shows the amount of responsibility provided in a typical Japanese-run North American operation, where employees are divided into production teams. The third column shows the amount of responsibility and authority provided in highly empowered U.S. organizations using self-directed work teams.

As suggested by Figure 10.2, employees in highly empowered North American organizations have considerably more authority and responsibility than employees in Japanese-run North American companies. Figure 10.2 also shows why Japanese companies initially seem attractive to many North Americans—they offer more authority and responsibility than traditional local employers. But for many North Americans, this attraction has started to fade because many Japanese companies have not been successful in moving in the direction of the highly empowered North American organization.

Empowerment in Japanese organizations differs in some very subtle, yet major, ways. In Japanese teams, employees often work together under strong and controlling managers. Those managers might exert control in subtle and indirect ways and seldom interfere, but their authority, nonetheless, is intended to be pervasive. By contrast, one goal of empowered teams in North American organizations is to eliminate the need for strong management authority—changing the role to that of a coach.

Not all North American organizations want to be highly empowered organizations, but the trend seems irrevocable. Even those companies that seemed firmly stuck at the lower end of the empowerment continuum (probably the great majority of North American companies) are beginning to buckle under the pressures to change. The trend to reduce management levels (flatten organizations) has become all but irreversible in North America. Just-in-time manufacturing and continuous improvement techniques borrowed from the Japanese are difficult, if not impossible, in supervisor-centered organizations, as many failed efforts have demonstrated. Hence, the push to decentralize power and give responsibility to worker teams who are closer to the work or customer, even in companies where labor-management relationships have traditionally been marked by extreme mistrust.

Can Japanese organizations in North America operate at Level 4 or 5 on the empowerment continuum? Do they want to?

The limits to empowerment in Japanese organizations are often deliberate yet unintentional:

- Language and cultural differences, which make empathy between Japanese and North Americans difficult, limit the amount of trust Japanese organizations might have in local employees. This makes it difficult to give local employees increased responsibilities.
- Japanese organizations might feel that it is necessary to maintain tight centralized control. This rules out any possibility of much local decision making.
- Japanese organizations can be empowering, but they are not *highly* empowering in a North American sense. Within certain boundaries, individual jobs and team responsibilities can be quite broad and flexible, but initiative beyond those boundaries is often discouraged. Perhaps Japanese organizations do not recognize a psychological need, acknowledged by many North American firms, to continually increase the feelings of empowerment among employees.
- Above all, empowerment depends on the skills and training of supervisors and others in contact with frontline employees. Japanese in positions of authority rarely have received any training. Many of their day-to-day actions in a North American organization—actions that might seem quite natural to Japanese employees—are distinctly *unempowering*.

STEPS TO CREATE EMPOWERMENT AND KEY PRINCIPLE 4

Empowerment is created by changing job responsibilities and authority, providing better communication about what is happening in the organization, and generally involving employees more in their work. It also is created by the employee's immediate supervisor. In many ways, the degree of empowerment felt by individuals is more a function of their supervisors' skills than anything the organization can do. A company can provide a highly empowered work situation, but if the immediate supervisor is controlling and autocratic, the employee feels very little empowerment. Conversely, even in a traditional, unempowered organization, where job duties are rigid and unchanging, a highly empowering supervisor who challenges employees to exhibit initiative and trusts and respects their judgments can provide employees with a considerable sense of empowerment.

An empowering leader uses the three leadership skills (key principles) discussed in Chapter 9: (1) maintain or enhance self-esteem; (2) listen and respond with empathy; (3) ask for help and encourage involvement. An empowering leader also uses the fourth key principle: (4) offer help without removing responsibility for action.

Our observations suggest that many supervisors and managers in Japanese organizations are ineffective in using the fourth key principle. A supervisor or advisor who rushes to an employee struggling with a problem and provides the solution is not using this principle. While managers everywhere are tempted to do this, the tendency seems especially pronounced among Japanese managers, supervisors, and advisors in North America.

In an empowered organization, managers and supervisors are careful to help employees solve problems, even if that takes longer or seems inefficient. The reason: The next time problems arise, employees will be better able to solve them without intervention. Plus, they will feel more job ownership and satisfaction.

The same approach is needed in handling ideas from employees. If a supervisor thanks an employee for a good idea and then goes on to research the idea further or even implement it, the supervisor has taken ownership of the idea from the employee, who was excited about showing initiative and being innovative. Because of the supervisor's action, the energy created from the excitement of the discovery evaporates.

An effective supervisor or manager uses Key Principle 4 by helping the employee work through and build on the original idea. At some point, the supervisor can coach the employee in making appropriate presentations of that idea to others in the organization to get cooperation or resources. Through this process, the employee maintains ownership for implementation of the idea and presents the idea to various involved groups within the organization. The pride and feelings of accomplishment resulting from that idea serve to energize and activate the employee to make the idea work.

The use of Key Principle 4 is an important but subtle skill, difficult for any leader to master. Unfortunately, many Japanese trainers and production coordinators, who are on the "front lines" in North America in terms of empowering local employees, often seem to be the ones most lacking in this skill. Many are experienced trainers, but they have little or no experience or training in using the key principles and have varying degrees of difficulty in communicating in English. These disadvantages frequently force them into a mode of "stop asking questions and just do it this way," which is easily interpreted as disrespect by North Americans. "Some Japanese advisors have such low expectations of U.S. workers that it drives the workers crazy," says an American manager, who adds, "When you take an American who might have had a similar production job for twenty years and say, 'This is a screwdriver, and we use it to put this screw into this slot,' it can be pretty insulting."

"Ironically, the model for empowering people comes from the Japanese," one American manager notes. "But it is obvious that when matched head-to-head against a cutting-edge American company, Japanese companies can't compete on empowerment." If empowerment is the linchpin of competitive success in the nineties—and we think it is—it could be one of the few examples of an idea borrowed from the Japanese that can be used against them effectively.

EMPOWERMENT AT THE MANAGEMENT LEVEL

North American managers, accustomed to responsibility and authority in North American organizations, find both dramatically curtailed in many Japanese companies. Virtually all the problems reported in this book, aside from the obvious cultural and communication differences, can be traced to North American managers feeling that they lack the information, knowledge, and decision-making responsibilities they had in previous jobs. Ironically, many of these same managers believe that they had been promised all of these things in their new positions with Japanese companies.

One major difference between North American managers and production employees is that while employees initially find the level of empowerment in Japanese companies refreshing, managers and professionals quickly start to chafe at what they see as a lack of empowerment. While employees might have been accustomed to little empowerment in previous jobs, managers coming into Japanese firms are coming from positions very high on any empowerment continuum. They are used to making important decisions, guiding their organizations, having wide access to information about their companies, and dealing with issues inside and outside the organization.

In their new positions with Japanese organizations, these managers find themselves in a very different situation: sliding down the empowerment scale. While some initial retreat in empowerment is common in almost any new job, managers expect to return to the previous, or higher, level very quickly. That is not what they find at many Japanese-owned firms.

One reason is a perceived lack of operational information. Information is the lifeblood of management to many North Americans, which is why local managers in Japanese companies find the limited information available to them on long-term objectives and plans especially vexing. "The Japanese tend to spoon-feed just enough information to keep you going another day," says an American manager. Because of language and communication barriers and little involvement in advanced planning or financial matters (senior financial positions usually are held exclusively by Japanese managers who communicate mostly with headquarters and not with local managers), a surprising number of senior North American managers say they don't even know if their operations are profitable or if goals or targets are being met.

Other managers cite their lack of clear, measurable performance goals (Chapter 11) and their lack of performance feedback (Chapter 12). "How can I feel good about myself or what I'm doing if I don't know what I'm expected to accomplish and how I'm doing relative to those targets?" said one manager. "You lose the thrill of the chase, and the exhilaration of accomplishment. It's taking the fun and the challenge out of my job!"

Some Japanese organizations seem to equate empowerment with abandonment of authority by Japanese management and the assumption of total independence by local employees and management. Concerns about control and knowledge of organizational operations are natural, but they could indicate a misunderstanding of empowerment. But empowerment does not mean abandonment or abdication of all authority. Senior leaders in any organization still need detailed knowledge of operations and must assert their influence when necessary. The distinction between empowering and unempowering leadership lies in how the subordinates feel about the ways leaders exert influence. Does the subordinate feel dictated to or coached? Does the subordinate understand the reason for the change or advice?

North American employees and managers don't mind keeping their superiors and others informed about what they are doing—they expect it. They recognize the need to share information to coordinate and integrate operations. Their problems come about when they perceive all the information flow is in one direction or that the information is being used to make decisions for them.

We feel that empowerment, as further defined in the next two chapters, is a necessary ingredient for Japanese organizations in North America. Without it, many key employees who possess significant organizational and technical knowledge will leave. Empowerment at the managerial level may require major organizational and operational changes in Japanese companies—changes that are often resisted. However, these changes will have to be made eventually if Japanese organizations hope to prosper with mixed Japanese and North American work forces. The most successful North American companies are providing employees at all levels with a great deal of the decision-making authority—considerably beyond the limits of most Japanese companies operating in North America. For Japanese companies to really turn on the inner power of their employees, and particularly their managers, after the challenge of the start-up has passed, they have to rethink personnel policies related to local responsibility and authority. Otherwise, continuous productivity improvement—the key to competing with highly empowered North American organizations—may prove an elusive goal.

EMPOWERMENT AT THE ORGANIZATIONAL LEVEL

Empowered organizations share fourteen factors. An audit of where an organization stands relative to these factors is a good starting place in creating an empowered organization.

No organization will be high in all fourteen factors. Even highly empowered organizations can't claim that distinction. The factors describe goals that organizations should strive to achieve.

Empowered organizations have:

• **Understanding, at all organizational levels, of the meaning of empowerment and how to achieve it.** Empowerment is a value or belief system, not a program. All levels of the organization must understand how empowerment can meet both personal and business needs and the actions needed to achieve it.

• **Well-understood and accepted vision and values to guide decision making.** An empowered organization supports decision making at the level closest to the job. To make good decisions, people need to have a clear understanding of the organization's direction—its vision (mission) and how they contribute to achieving it. They also need to understand the organization's basic values, which can act as guidelines for decision making.

• **Performance management systems that provide clear understanding of job responsibilities and methods for measuring success.** Empowered employees and leaders work together to develop a clear understanding of job responsibilities, limits of authority, and methods for measuring success. To ensure optimum performance, individuals need to know how their goals and performance expectations link to the overall objectives of the team, the department, and the business strategy of the organization. They also need continuous feedback on their performance, suggestions for improvement, and coaching for success.

• **Jobs designed to provide ownership and responsibility.** Empowerment must be built into employees' jobs. Tasks must be defined so that people have responsibility for a meaningful process or output, can make decisions and commit appropriate organizational resources,

continued

and can continually measure their own successes. Empowered employees have the time, knowledge, and resources to achieve success.

• **Effective communication about the organization's plans, successes, and failures.** Empowered employees want to know about the organization's plans, successes, and failures. Truthful and up-to-date communication ensures that employees identify with the organization and actively contribute to its success. When employees understand the organization's direction, they are more likely to support its actions.

• **Reward and recognition systems that build pride and self-esteem.** Empowered employees have an inherent sense of pride in their accomplishments and contributions to the organization. Psychological and tangible recognition programs can enhance these feelings. Compensation and other reward systems need to be in sync with the empowered organization's values. Often these systems need to become more team-oriented in their recognition of job performance and specific accomplishments.

• **Selection and promotion systems to identify quality workers and leaders.** Some people are more interested than others in becoming empowered. Placing individuals with appropriate motivations and skills in an empowered environment increases the likelihood that the benefits of empowerment will be achieved in a more timely and cost-effective manner. Also, an organization's selection and promotion choices can communicate its commitment to empowerment.

• **Organizational systems, such as information systems and travel-reimbursement policies.** Other organizational systems—information systems, travel-reimbursement policies, career-planning procedures, succession planning, discipline, personnel policies, tuition refund policy, quality circles, and suggestion systems—can either instill people with a sense of power or make them feel as if they have none.

• **Empowering leadership/training.** Leaders have tremendous impact on the degree of empowerment their employees feel. Through the tasks they delegate, the control they exert, the initiative they encourage, and the feedback and reinforcement they provide, empowering leaders not only encourage empowerment but also build employee confidence. By coaching for success and helping employees feel ownership of their ideas, leaders ensure employees' dedication and com-

continued

mitment to their work. Enhancement of leadership skills is an ongoing process as employees and teams move toward increased empowerment.

• **Job and technical skills/training.** In an empowered organization, employees take on additional tasks and often rotate jobs. They need to understand not only how to do their own jobs but also every job on their team. They might be required to learn statistical process control or their company's budgetary process. Technical and job training prepares employees for these new responsibilities. Nothing is more empowering than providing employees with skills training to do their jobs well.

• **Interpersonal and problem-solving skills/training.** Empowered employees, as individuals or in teams, interact more often with co-workers, suppliers, customers, and management. They are expected to identify problems and opportunities and take appropriate actions. Empowered employees must be able to lead others and resolve their own conflicts without appealing to higher authority. Skills training usually is needed as employees and teams assume more responsibilities.

• **Frontline customer service skills/training.** Empowered organizations focus on customer service skills because their frontline people represent the organization to the customer. Customers' perceptions of an organization develop from the treatment they receive from customer contact people. An empowered organization provides the training that frontline service people need to meet and exceed their customers' expectations.

• **Empowering support groups/training.** Like leaders, support group personnel—engineering, accounting, training—can help frontline employees build a sense of job ownership and responsibility. Ongoing training and management support are required to help them assume these new roles. Support personnel who effectively coach, reinforce, and offer help without taking responsibility build employee confidence and skill. Empowered employees gradually handle more of the support groups' responsibilities. Ultimately, an effective support group evolves from doers into trainers and coaches, viewing others as their partners.

continued

• **Work teams.** Increasingly, organizations empower by encouraging teams and teamwork—cross-functional quality action teams, customer-focused groups, and integrated product development teams. A special type of team—the self-directed work team—organizes individuals so that they are responsible for a given area or output. The team takes on many responsibilities previously assigned to supervisors, such as job assignments, product quality, selection of new members, and sometimes even performance evaluation. A self-directed work team is an excellent way to empower individuals whose current jobs are limited in scope.

People feel empowered when they have clear job responsibilities, can continuously measure their own successes, are part of teams that make meaningful decisions about work activities, and are supported by supervisors and staff that offer help (coach) without taking away job responsibility. These are not easy goals, but they are achievable—as shown by many organizations that are winning the competitiveness race.

ALL-AMERICAN SUCCESS STORIES

Many North American organizations have reached very high levels of quality, customer service, and productivity through consistent efforts to provide a greater sense of empowerment to employees. A number of North American success stories were reported in the book *Empowered Teams*. Notable examples include:

• At Aid Association for Lutherans (AAL), teams do their own interviewing and make hiring decisions. AAL reports that by dividing its entire work force into multiskilled teams, productivity has increased by 20 percent. Before, the company had a single-function, assembly-line approach to assigning tasks. Now, team members learn as many as twenty different service-related jobs. One result: The company has been able to cut personnel by 10 percent while handling 10 percent more transactions. Another insurance company, Shenan-
continued

doah Life, used empowered teams to reduce staff and increase the volume of work handled by 33 percent.

• At Lake Superior Paper Industries, teams handle their own work scheduling, work assignments, and holiday and vacation planning. In its first year of being team-run, the company had predicted a $17-million loss, but instead made $3 million on revenues of $111 million due to productivity gains.

• At Johnsonville Foods, a sausage company in Wisconsin, sales rose from $4 million to $150 million after an eight-year process of refashioning the company to be run by highly empowered teams. One pivotal event was the decision by team members to take on a large and lucrative outside order. Managers feared the order would upset production schedules and affect quality but kept to its commitment to let the teams make such decisions. The teams managed to schedule the work, uphold quality standards, and gain valuable experience in successfully handling larger volumes of work. Similarly, seven self-directed, eleven-person teams at the Schreiber Foods cheese factory in Arizona now produce a million pounds of cheese a week—twice as much as other cheese factories its size.

• Several major American corporations that use empowered teams at selected sites report that team-based facilities are vastly more productive than traditional facilities. General Mills' plants that use teams are 40 percent more productive than plants that operate without teams. General Electric's Salisbury, North Carolina, plant increased productivity by 250 percent compared to GE plants building the same products without teams. Goodyear Tire and Rubber adopted a team approach for its Lawton, Oklahoma, facility and gave teams broad responsibilities. The change enabled the plant to operate with 35 percent fewer managers and produce 50,000 tires per day compared with 25,000 at a similar plant.

11

PERFORMANCE MANAGEMENT:

WHAT NORTH AMERICANS WANT

*I don't have any idea about what I am really responsible for,
except in the broadest sense. I don't know what I am supposed to
accomplish, and thus I can't tell how I am doing. It's very
frustrating.*

AMERICAN MANAGER

*The best way of meeting the role-clarity needs of American
managers is a good performance management system—but the
Japanese won't have any of it.*

AMERICAN MANAGER

A NORTH AMERICAN NECESSITY

THE QUESTIONS NORTH AMERICANS want answered seem simple on the
surface: *What's expected of me? How am I doing? How can I improve?*
A system that helps employees answer these questions is usually

126

called a performance management system in North America.* As we define it in programs we have developed, performance management consists of defining job responsibilities and setting measurable goals, providing day-to-day feedback and coaching regarding progress toward those goals, and reviewing achievement of goals through an annual performance appraisal.

These are not easy skills for managers to master, but many North American companies have recognized that these skills are vital to the effective development of their human resources. In fact, many North American companies provide managers with extensive skill-building training in each of these areas.

Japanese organizations have thrived without the performance management systems that North American employees virtually take for granted. Japanese employees within Japanese organizations do, of course, have ways of assessing their performance and progress and receiving performance feedback from superiors. But the purpose and implementation of performance management in Japanese organizations differ in several key areas from the performance management typically practiced in North American organizations. As we've suggested, these differences give the Japanese organization its great competitive strength, but they also leave Japanese managers unprepared for the realities of the North American workplace.

What are some of these differences? As we have noted, in a typical Japanese company, jobs are less clearly defined, and hardly ever defined with formal job descriptions because the objective is more often team performance than individual performance. "One's job responsibility is always ambiguous or floating," says a Japanese manager. "Jobs are adjusted continuously to meet changing situations." Managers like that because it gives them great flexibility in assigning tasks. It also makes employees more flexible in what they are willing—and able—to do. Because jobs are not clearly defined, it can be hard to establish specific goals for employees. Even if goals are established, Japanese organizations might be so responsive to changes

* We should note that this is in some ways a misleading term because it implies that a manager is managing a subordinate's performance. Ideally, a manager helps the subordinate to define what's important and to set objectives. The subordinate then manages his or her performance on their own. A better term might be "enabling performance" or "defining what's important."

in their environments that employee goals are frequently changed. One Japanese manager sums up the purpose of it all: "Japanese companies want workers available at any time for any job requirement."

The Japanese approach to job duties and individual performance goals makes the North American-style performance appraisal discussion relatively unimportant and even superfluous. Cultural rules that emphasize discretion and indirect communication to preserve harmony and maintain the "face" of others also discourage direct, unambiguous performance evaluations in Japanese organizations. Japanese employees have many ways to gauge how well they meet goals and how their career is progressing, but rarely is a one-on-one performance evaluation meeting with their immediate supervisor one of them.

One Japanese researcher informally surveyed Japanese professionals and found that while many had yearly performance reviews, they were all characterized as "formalities" that served little more than symbolic purposes. Employees in several major Japanese corporations said they were unaware of anyone *ever* receiving formal performance reviews in their companies. Performance feedback took place informally—over drinks after work—or was determined by subtle differences in annual salary increases or by "interpreting" the words and gestures of supervisors or managers. Employees sensitive to these signals and their meanings saw little need for a more formal process. Most felt it was important to be able to sense the expectations of their managers without having those expectations clearly stated. Employees who had developed a good set of antennae when it came to understanding what kept the boss happy had a clear road ahead of them.

Japanese managers' relative unfamiliarity with performance management practices in Western organizations can be a great disadvantage to them in North America. Our research suggests that clear performance objectives are rare for North Americans in many Japanese workplaces in North America—perhaps in the majority of them. Seldom do North American managers and their Japanese colleagues or superiors have informal, face-to-face performance evaluations. Formal performance evaluations (see Chapter 12) can be nonexistent.

The challenge facing Japanese organizations is twofold: First, distinctly non-Japanese performance management systems must be created. Second, Japanese organizations may need to do a *better* job of performance management than typical North American companies. Better because the lack of organizational transparency, coupled with cultural differences and communication problems, creates so many opportunities for ambiguity and confusion to creep into the Japanese organization in North America. This makes it much harder to provide the clarity and direction North Americans need.

It should be noted that many North American firms do a very poor job of meeting their employees' expectations in defining job responsibilities and goals and in providing accurate performance feedback. In fact, the clarity of goals and quality of performance feedback regularly receive the lowest marks in job satisfaction, according to opinion surveys conducted by North American companies. However, North American companies are usually not indifferent to the problem. Many have had great success in changing employee perceptions by using performance management systems and training managers to use them effectively. Often the manager's ability to use performance management skills with subordinates is an integral part of the manager's own performance assessment.

THE FIRST CHALLENGE: SETTING KEY RESULT AREAS

North Americans at all levels want to know what they are accountable for in their jobs. In other words, what key results—specific outputs or end results that contribute to an organization's performance—are expected of them? In an ideal situation, an individual's key results are linked to the work unit's key results, which in turn are linked to the organization's business objectives. Coordinating key results at all levels is integral to moving the organization in the direction desired by top management. There is a popular cliché in American organizations, one unfortunately rooted in reality: People work very hard, but often on the wrong things. Having clear key result areas keeps people from working on the wrong things.

In more progressive and empowering North American companies, employees, supervisors, and managers draft the key result areas for their own positions. Then they modify or finalize them in consultation with other team members and their leader. In training programs, employees at all levels learn how to define their key result areas, and managers learn how to coach their subordinates through the process.

Because Japanese employees are far more comfortable with fluid key result areas, Japanese managers are often struck by the dramatic differences in North America. "Here, responsibilities are used as ways to draw lines that can't be crossed," comments one Japanese manager disdainfully. "Their attitude seems to be 'Keep out. Don't invade my responsibilities.' And if they don't perceive it to be their responsibility, they don't think they have to worry about it. It's someone else's problem."

Not all employees encountered by Japanese managers in North America will be that rigid, nor should the performance management system. Flexibility is an attribute of both a good performance management system and good employees. Key result areas should be considered guides—not immutable rules. When jobs change, the key result areas need to be revised.

Many Japanese companies shun the task of setting key result areas. "We've discovered that in many ways Japanese companies are just positively, absolutely, anti-key result areas," says an American executive who has worked for several Japanese companies on plant start-ups:

> They believe in flexible boundaries. If someone is real bright and shows initiative, he might spill over into my job, or I might spill over into his, or we might both spill over into someone else's job. While it might look chaotic to some Americans, it allows Japanese companies to have a whole lot of people at the same pay doing vastly different jobs of vastly different importance. With their better intuitive sense of what the organization wants from them, Japanese employees can cope and even thrive on the uncertainty.
>
> But that same amorphous quality could prevent Japanese companies from confronting performance and personnel issues that have a major impact in North America. It could be their Achilles' heel. We've concluded that with plant start-ups, you've got to look at key result areas every six months because the situation is so dynamic. But the inability of some Japanese managers to get comfortable with this means that you have people running around long after an operation gets going who don't have a clear idea of what they're supposed to be doing.

The need for clear key result areas can be interpreted by Japanese managers as another tiresome instance of North American egotism.

"It's all too easy to see this constant concern for 'what's my role' in this and that as a kind of selfishness," says a Japanese manager with several years of U.S. experience. He adds that, from his perspective, there is indeed a certain element of selfishness to it. "But," he adds, "it also shows great concern for being respected by the company for doing a good job." Most Japanese managers, upon reflection, reach a similar conclusion. Most are aware that North American workers typically want to do a good job and will work hard if properly motivated. Unfortunately, this manager admits, Japanese personnel are often too easily blinded by what they consider the egotistical aspect of the North American employee's search for role clarity.

Many North Americans today are not seeking the old hierarchy of rigid management levels. They like the increasing use of cross-functional teams and other means of creating more flexible, more responsible organizations. But, they still feel the need to be sure that their idea of what's important is the same as their boss's and that they mutually agree on goals and measurement methods. Participation on a specific team can be a legitimate key result area and its success a personal, measurable goal. North Americans working in self-directed work teams also are willingly adjusting to the increasing use of team key result areas and appraisals. Managers and employees are willing to adjust to new appraisal systems, just as they have adjusted to new organizational structures.

IDENTIFYING PERFORMANCE OBJECTIVES

After key result areas are established, North Americans need to set measurable objectives (goals or targets) in each key result area. Good objectives have the following characteristics:

• **They're measurable.** Japanese managers sometimes say they establish objectives with vague parameters ("as quickly as possible," "spend no more than you have to," and so on) to ensure that employees explore every possible option. By being precise about measurements or telling employees exactly what is expected, Japanese managers fear they run the risk of limiting employees' initiative to seek the best solutions on their own. But when North Americans encounter vagueness in Japanese organizations, the results can be frustrating.

Consider the story of an American engineer who quit her job at a Japanese manufacturing facility in the Midwest because of a lack of measurable direction. Her reaction might indeed seem egocentric and even childish by Japanese standards, but it's a telling example of how many North Americans think.

I was given a major project by a Japanese production engineer, and while I felt good about this display of trust, I couldn't pin him down about what he wanted. I hadn't been there long enough to make certain decisions myself, and I suppose I bothered him about things like the amount of money I could spend and when he needed it done. Finally, I said, "Look, I really can't do this without a budget and a timetable." He was genuinely surprised. "Don't you know?" he said. "Your budget is as little as possible, your timetable as soon as possible." I suppose that has a sort of Zen-like simplicity, but it's a complete wash as a management principle as far as I'm concerned. There's just too much to learn in a new operation like this and just too little effort given to help you learn it. Eventually you can start feeling apprehensive about trying anything at all.

• **They're controllable.** To North Americans, if the results objectives of their positions are to be perceived as fair and realistic, they need the resources and authority to make them happen.

• **They're time-bound.** People need to know how much time they have to meet a results objective. That's probably universal. But North Americans want exact dates, not "as soon as possible."

• **They're realistic.** Both North Americans and Japanese value challenge in their jobs and will stretch to meet high expectations, but unrealistic results objectives are frustrating and discouraging. Having the individual set his or her own objectives (to be reviewed by the manager) is an excellent way of assuring realistic objectives.

COACHING AND REINFORCING PERFORMANCE

Helping subordinates set key result areas and identify performance objectives is only part of the job of the effective manager. A tracking system is needed to allow both the manager and the subordinate to determine how actual performance compares with those objectives.

Self-tracking of achievements toward performance objectives is an important attribute of empowerment. Good results provide the pride and satisfaction that come from accomplishment. Poor results provide guidance for further effort. Managers also need to track performance to identify problems and help individuals correct them quickly, reward accomplishments, and recognize and reinforce added effort.

Coaching and reinforcing tracked performance, not haphazardly or sporadically, but on a systematic, frequent basis, are two more essential leadership skills necessary for effective performance management. Japanese managers in North America seem to have both unique strengths and weaknesses in this area. One difference between Japanese and North American managers has to do with the very definitions and purposes of coaching, and especially reinforcing performance. First, we'll look at coaching.

Coaching, as we define it, is distinct from training, which is a process of creating a skill where no skill existed. Coaching is also distinct from performance reviews and appraisals, which usually are yearly events intended to review achievement related to goals and often are mandated by company policy. Coaching happens every day. It can be deliberate and purposeful, or unplanned and spontaneous. In its broadest sense, coaching is the act of discussing ideas and plans with individuals, helping them build and shape those ideas and plans, and then helping them move in the direction of desired outcomes. "It means helping, facilitating, clearing the way, testing ideas, and guiding," says an American manager.

To be most effective, coaching should be applied in a way that allows the employee to retain responsibility for ideas and implementation, no matter how much information, expertise, and guidance the manager provides. Otherwise, the manager is telling the person to do something and how to do it, not giving him or her the skill and confidence to do it. This is reflected in Key Principle 4 (discussed in Chapter 10): "Offer help without removing responsibility for action." In this sense, coaching is really a form of empowerment.

An important aspect of coaching in North American organizations is coaching for success rather than merely correcting errors. While mistakes provide valuable lessons, North Americans learn more effectively when managers help them understand how to do a task right the first time. Thus, effective North American managers are those who work with individuals during assignments, not after they are completed. Effective coaching, in fact, tends to be participative, with a certain amount of give and take between a manager and the individual being coached.

"Coaching, as the Japanese practice it, is so different from our perspective and expectations that you can't expect it to work," says one American manager with many years of experience working for Japanese companies. Why not?

Japanese managers like to test subordinates by pushing them to develop solutions to problems themselves. They feel that a manager's involvement is most appropriate when it's time to review proposed solutions to problems, not the problems themselves. As one Japanese manager in Ohio explains:

> In North America, the good manager says, "If you have a problem, come see me. My door is always open." So what happens? Everyone goes to see him and his time is inappropriately spent. A Japanese manager would hope instead to create a situation where everyone pursues their own responsibilities and, instead of coming to you with problems, comes to you with proposed solutions. The problem itself is the subordinate's concern.

While this approach is good in theory, in practice it can be quite frustrating to North Americans, who are more likely to want to explore problems with their managers and colleagues and to work on solutions together.

One key coaching problem any manager faces is handling poor ideas from subordinates. When a subordinate comes up with a good idea, the manager's job is to work with that individual on perfecting the idea and implementing it. It's a different matter when a subordinate seems committed to an idea that a manager feels is flawed or unworkable. How do you tell the individual the idea won't work without harming his or her commitment to solving the problem, or making the individual reluctant to bring you other ideas?

Skill in handling such situations is not easily mastered by managers, but it can be developed through training—specifically through training that helps managers apply the key principles on a consistent and daily basis. In this situation, maintaining self-esteem, listening and responding with empathy, and above all, *questioning* in a way that helps the individual see the flaws in his or her thinking without having them directly pointed out, is essential. This takes time but is worth the effort. Individuals learn to evaluate their decisions more effectively and are more likely to develop better decisions in the future. They also feel some pride in discovering their own mistakes and are not demotivated by having their ideas rejected or changed by others. They keep ownership of the problem and are motivated to seek other solutions.

In North America, a variety of coaching strategies seem to work, and the benefits of applying them in a formal and systematic way inside Japanese-owned companies seem obvious. For one, North American managers might not feel as estranged from their environment if they are given clear and understandable coaching and reinforcement in terms that, culturally, they've learned to respond to. From the Japanese manager's perspective, a systematic approach to coaching will build communication and trust faster and, of course, greatly improve the manager's chances of successfully completing his North American assignment.

If coaching for success provides the means for developing effective performance, reinforcement is the glue that makes the performance stick. Coaching and reinforcing are interrelated. Once coaching has helped an individual successfully perform an action, reinforcement will help cement the behavior. Reinforcement is also an important part of enhancing self-esteem.

By reinforcement, we mean the deliberate effort by a manager to praise the use of specific skills and/or actions—not just praise for accomplishing a task or meeting a goal. Accomplishing a task or meeting a goal can take weeks, months, or even years. Reinforcement loses much of its effectiveness, and sometimes even its purpose, if managers wait until the results are in. That's why most effective North American managers reinforce individuals at intermediate points along the way, primarily by reinforcing the behaviors or skills needed to accomplish a task. For example, a manager might praise a subordinate's planning skills after reviewing various documents related to a major project, even though the project might not be completed for months.

Using specific praise to reinforce performance is a difficult skill for Japanese managers in North America to develop, due to difficulties in using English and the diminished roles that praise and reinforcement play in the Japanese workplace. "There might be a lot of truth to the

feeling that we don't know how to respond to individual performance," one Japanese manager admits, adding:

> Our feeling is that individuals should be motivated from within. Teams
> must be developed from without. We might even feel that praising
> individuals can damage team development. But in North America,
> people tend to think in individual terms, not group terms, and while
> they can work quite well together as teams, people must feel individu-
> ally motivated. We might feel that commendable actions of individuals
> don't merit special attention, since people who perform well are only
> doing what they're supposed to be doing. If we notice anything, it is
> defects in performance, not excellent examples of performance. We
> know how to say, "Here's what's wrong; here's how to correct it," but
> are less successful saying, "Here's why what you did is so good."

WHOSE RESPONSIBILITY IS IT?

Japanese managers in North America quickly notice other basic differences between managing performance in Japan and North America. Some of the things they need to do to be effective managers in
North America run counter to the Japanese notion of managing. In
fact, performance management as we've described it, with its emphasis on explicit (but not controlling) direction and ongoing coaching
by managers, can be rather surprising to Japanese managers.

In Japan, after all, it is more often subordinates who make the
effort to determine their superiors' intentions and guess the direction
of the company—both of which rarely have to be spelled out. Managers feel less need to shape employee behavior, because employees
are careful to make their behavior conform to management's often
unstated wishes. It takes a great deal of time and effort—Japanese
managers in North America come to realize—to coach, help employees think through problems, listen and respond with empathy,
track progress, and apply praise and reinforcement when needed.
"That managers should make such exhaustive efforts is rather surprising," says one Japanese manager, who wonders how managers in
North America actually find time to manage.

We feel such efforts need to be made, however, if North Americans
are to perform to their full potential. More effort to reinforce performance is an especially important need, because Japanese managers

are closely watched by the North Americans they work with. The opinions of Japanese managers will be respected and their approval sought, especially when North Americans feel they're achieving performance expectations or are successfully using skills and behaviors the organization has targeted as necessary. Perceptions that their efforts are received with indifference create morale and commitment problems that tend to persist and, in some Japanese organizations, have proved impossible to erase without reassigning Japanese personnel.

12

FACING THE CHALLENGE:

PERFORMANCE APPRAISALS

In Japan, there's this convoluted way of finding out how you're doing in a company. You and your buddies get together and find out how much of a raise each of you got. No one gets that much more than anyone else, but there are subtle distinctions. If I got this much and you got that much, then I can look at our level in the company, calculate a few other ratios, and figure out who is more highly regarded. That, strange as it seems, is how the Japanese give performance feedback.

AMERICAN MANAGER

Performance is reviewed, but it's painfully face-saving and non-confrontational. The information content—the "here's how we think you're doing and here's how we can work together to keep your performance improving"—can be virtually nonexistent. Japanese managers just don't like formalized systems that force them to confront issues. That's why they don't like performance appraisals.

AMERICAN MANAGER

THERE IS NO EQUIVALENT of a North American-style performance review in most Japanese organizations, and in Japan, at least, there might be little need for one. The differences between the North American and Japanese approaches to performance reviews are fundamental. These start with the absence of formal key result areas, performance measurement methods, and goals, which means there is no baseline for evaluating employee performance in many Japanese organizations. In North American organizations, however, key result areas and measurable goals are frequently used as the starting point for employee evaluations. Moreover, criteria used to evaluate job performance are frequently subjective in Japan, whereas objectivity is an important quality in North American performance evaluations.

Japanese managers, for example, might be measured by their ability to get along, their spirit, and their imagination. They might rarely see written evaluations. For "official" feedback, managers often receive form letters, little different from letters that other managers receive. And while evaluations do affect salaries and promotions, Japanese managers often say they really find out if they're doing well by the number of challenging special assignments they receive. Less-capable managers get routine tasks of dwindling importance and might eventually be reduced to virtual irrelevancy with no subordinates or authority.

FORMAL PERFORMANCE APPRAISALS

The situation is very different in North America, where organizations feel that employees need detailed and well-documented appraisals of their job performance. These appraisals usually are done on an annual basis, although some organizations conduct performance reviews more frequently. A written document summarizing the appraisal is often discussed in a one-on-one meeting between an employee and his or her immediate superior. Performance appraisal discussions are seen as a key method for helping individuals correct deficiencies, improve their performance, or live up to their potential. The performance appraisal meeting covers performance results (customer service, output, quality, productivity, sales, etc.) and on-the-job behavior. This might include how well a manager coached and developed his or her subordinates, or how an individual functioned as a member of a team.

There are also important legal implications. In the United States and Canada, if you want to fire an employee or take disciplinary action, it is important to document a series of meetings with that employee in which specific performance problems were discussed. Otherwise, fired or disciplined employees might claim in a lawsuit that other factors, such as age, race, or gender, were behind the action. The annual performance appraisal report is an important part of documenting deterioration in performance. One sure way to guarantee a lawsuit in America is to fire someone over poor performance when that person has a recent positive performance evaluation in the personnel file.

Several Japanese companies learned that lesson when they issued performance review letters that contained perfunctory "form letter" praise to North American managers and later laid off the same managers. While the companies might have been legitimately dissatisfied with the fired managers' performances, the managers simply pointed out that the letters contained language such as, "We value your commitment and skill," and "We are pleased with your superior efforts." The managers filed suit, charging discrimination based on national origin. "The letters said we performed well," the fired North American managers claimed. "So why were we fired?"

As increasing numbers of North American managers report to them directly, Japanese managers are confronting the tough challenge of these and other performance management issues. So far, many report it has not been easy to adjust to the needs of their North American subordinates. One Japanese manager expresses this frustration:

> We approach performance appraisals quite differently. We want to look at earnestness in handling assignments, devotion to the job, and contributions to the total effort rather than individual achievements—all things that are hard to quantify in the way Americans desire. And even if employees achieve all goals 100 percent, I wonder if many Japanese managers will ever allow themselves to be satisfied. If you provide detailed information to employees on how you think they are doing, will that cause them to slack off and take things for granted? Close discussion is required before goals are established, but close discussion can prove very hard.

One result of these difficulties, this Japanese manager says, is that Japanese managers avoid performance evaluations of North

Americans entirely. Instead, they ask a North American to conduct perfunctory performance evaluations of other North Americans. When that happens, the effects can be very damaging. By avoiding performance reviews with American subordinates, Japanese managers isolate themselves from key parts of the performance management process. A divided organization results, with separate reporting channels limiting meaningful management contact between Japanese and North Americans. While this can provide a comfortable psychological distance for Japanese managers, it negates the possibility of a truly integrated or "blended" organization. Many Japanese managers with years of experience in North America are realizing that such a pattern is becoming increasingly untenable.

PRESCRIPTION: A NORTH AMERICAN MODEL FOR PERFORMANCE APPRAISAL DISCUSSIONS

Effective managers assess, review, and provide feedback on the performance of subordinates every day. The purpose of the formal, annual performance appraisal discussion is to complete a cyclical process that begins with the identification of key result areas and goals and continues with tracking, coaching, and reinforcing. The cycle begins again by using the results of the performance appraisal discussion to check the appropriateness of the key result areas and to establish new performance expectations. Figure 12.1 shows how the three parts meld into one another.

The formal performance appraisal discussion serves as the end and the beginning of a performance management system. The analysis of past performance provides the basis for the next set of performance expectations. This closes the loop of the ongoing performance cycle so that individuals know what is expected of them and what they need to do to achieve results in each performance period. Furthermore, the organization knows what results it can expect from each employee and what resources are needed to help them achieve those results.

The performance appraisal meeting is intended to review

continued

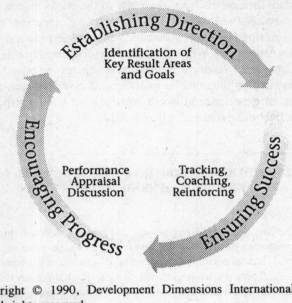

FIGURE 12.1
CLOSING THE LOOP

Establishing Direction

Identification of
Key Result Areas
and Goals

Encouraging Progress

Ensuring Success

Performance
Appraisal
Discussion

Tracking,
Coaching,
Reinforcing

actual performance data against previously established expectations, showing the individual, among other things, how performance affects pay and what steps the employee might need to take to meet personal goals within the company. Reinforcing performance that met or exceeded expectations is an important part of the meeting, as is encouraging an open discussion about performance problems and other job-related issues.

If an employee feels that he or she is being evaluated unfairly, the manager should be prepared to explain the reasons for the evaluation ratings and to support them with specific performance data. Managers must be careful to avoid debating their evaluations and, instead, focus the discussion on ways to improve performance. The employee will be satisfied with the meeting if he or she:

continued

- Understands the reasons for the manager's assessment.
- Knows the manager recognized performance that met or exceeded expectations.
- Understands how his or her performance affects pay.
- Believes the manager helped identify ways to improve performance.

In reality, the appraisal discussion itself is not all that important. Rather, it serves as a tool to accomplish two primary goals—goals that Japanese managers might feel happen naturally with Japanese employees but that need planned and deliberate encouragement in North America. These two goals are:

1. **Recognizing a specific level of performance achieved by an individual within the period covered.** The individual expects some type of recognition. This recognition makes the second important goal of performance appraisals possible, as described in the next point.

2. **Instilling in the individual a sense of commitment and motivation that will produce a consistently high level of performance in the future.**

Successful performance appraisal discussions generally are dependent on several important elements or traits. Among them are the following:

- **Lack of surprises.** Employees (frontline or managerial) need a clear idea of what will be discussed and why, the format and duration of the discussion, and a copy of an appraisal form that lists the areas on which they will be evaluated so they can prepare for the meeting.

As we've suggested, North Americans need and expect well-defined job expectations, or key result areas, which is why helping individuals set these key result areas is such an important part of a manager's duties. Moreover, North Americans need a clear understanding of the level of accomplishment, or objectives, expected of them. The performance appraisal meeting should be used to discuss these—and only these—well-understood key result areas and objectives. One of the biggest mistakes a manager can make during a performance appraisal discussion is to veer off in unexpected directions and discuss perfor-

continued

mance areas that the employee is unprepared to talk about or feels is an unimportant part of the job. When that happens, the performance appraisal meeting can become confusing and intimidating instead of being a constructive morale- and performance-building process.

Key result areas and objectives are rarely etched in stone and can be changed and adjusted throughout the year. But these changes must be made in collaboration with the employee so that even if an employee's performance expectations change dramatically during the year, discussion of the changes comes as no surprise during a performance appraisal discussion.

• **Based on data.** Most organizations use some type of performance appraisal form that guides the evaluation. Whatever its format, the evaluation provided should be based on data the manager has gathered throughout the year. A common mistake is to base the year's appraisal only on what the individual did during the last two weeks of the appraisal period. This happens because managers don't keep good records. Data for appraisal discussions can come from notes taken in staff meetings, direct observation, reports submitted by the employee, and many other sources. Objective data are important to give the employee a sense of objectivity and impartiality. They show employees the reasons for their evaluation. The data have legal implications as well, since they can be used to show that personnel decisions are not made arbitrarily or unfairly.

• **Positive interaction.** A manager's "style" in conducting a performance appraisal discussion will influence the outcome much more than the performance appraisal form. Employees will approach a performance appraisal meeting with a certain amount of anxiety. Their concerns might include a fear of being judged, a misunderstanding of the purpose and benefits of the appraisal, or resentment caused by anticipation that it will be "the manager's word against mine," with no opportunity for a rebuttal or defense.

Effective managers help overcome these concerns by encouraging questions and participation in the performance appraisal process and discussion. The meeting should be a positive experience for both parties. Performance that met or exceeded expectations should be praised. It is important not to make the mistake of minimizing accomplishments and focusing primarily on shortcomings. Equally important

continued

is devoting sufficient time to accomplishments since they are the high point of the employee's performance and represent a performance level you want the employee to continue achieving. Too often, positive performance is quickly highlighted as managers rush forward and spend most of the time on problems. Whenever possible, managers should apply the key principles of leadership (see Chapter 9) to show that they care about the employees and that they are holding the discussion for the employees' benefit.

• **Self-appraisal.** Often, North American managers give employees the chance to appraise their own performance and use the self-appraisal as the foundation of the performance review process. In such situations, employees complete the performance appraisal forms on their own. The appraisal discussion consists of comparing the self-appraisal with the manager's appraisal. This has a number of benefits:

• It encourages individuals to look objectively at their own jobs.

• It represents an opportunity for individuals to think about enhancement or corrective action plans away from the stress associated with the actual performance appraisal meeting.

• It reinforces the participatory aspect of the performance appraisal meeting. It is seen as a shared endeavor to help individuals continuously improve.

Some North American companies take self-appraisals a step further by employing a type of self-initiated performance management system in which individuals assume major responsibility for identifying their own key result areas and establishing objectives within those areas. While the key result areas and objectives are reviewed with the individual's manager, often only minor changes are made because individuals tend to set very high targets for themselves. The performance appraisal meeting becomes a process of individuals sharing their self-ratings and the boss adding comments and additional insights. They then reach an agreement on a final performance rating for each key result area. Many North Americans find this to be the easiest and most constructive way to conduct performance appraisals because it shifts the burden to employees, who generally respond to the process with a great deal of realism and objectivity. Some North American organizations like to

continued

say that managers never have more than one performance appraisal to complete—their own.

We have found that a self-appraisal system works very well in a Japanese organization because it shifts most of the burden of setting key result areas and goals, as well as reviewing progress, to the individual. When the North American handles most of the process, the Japanese boss can concentrate on constructive feedback and coaching.

• **Well-documented.** Regardless of who is most in control of the performance appraisal process—the employee or the manager—the results of the meeting must be documented thoroughly. This documentation usually consists of a memo or a form drafted or filled out by the manager or employee and signed by both. It is a way of assuring that both parties agree on what was decided, and it also gives the organization some legal protection should an employee ever make a charge of unfair treatment.

EASIER SAID THAN DONE?

How much challenge does conducting performance appraisal discussions present to typical Japanese managers? A big one, most North American managers who have worked with Japanese managers assert. It requires the use of objective criteria, with all employees evaluated against similar standards, not the more subjective measures that Japanese managers find useful. Many North American managers report that abandoning this subjective orientation toward performance evaluation is resisted by Japanese managers. Japanese managers also have trouble getting used to the idea of clear and detailed key result areas, which, as we've suggested, can run counter to the belief that job requirements should be kept as flexible and fluid as possible. But some Japanese managers find that thinking about and drafting key result areas and goals is a useful exercise. It helps them think like typical North American employees and understand the things that are important to them, especially the need for clarity and useful feedback on how well performance meets expectations.

Language is a major hurdle. Many Japanese managers might feel that conducting performance appraisals in English is simply beyond their abilities. Yet, if Japanese managers want to manage in a direct and unambiguous way, which is what most North Americans say they desperately want, some involvement in the performance management process and the performance appraisal discussion, in particular, is a minimum requirement.

Effectively evaluating an individual and communicating appraisal information are learned skills. Japanese managers might never feel at ease conducting appraisal meetings; nevertheless, they can be very effective—as proven by the many Japanese managers who have mastered these skills.

PART THREE

DEVELOPING THE JAPANESE ORGANIZATION IN NORTH AMERICA

13

ORGANIZATIONAL FIT:

HIRING RIGHT FOR THE JAPANESE-NORTH AMERICAN ENVIRONMENT

Japanese managers are amazingly perceptive at judging applicants. I don't know how they do it with their limited English—but they do it. They would be great with some training.

AMERICAN MANAGER

When evaluating job candidates it is easy for us to get fooled.

JAPANESE MANAGER

STAFFING: SUCCESS FROM BELOW

RECRUITING AND HIRING is another major challenge facing Japanese organizations in North America. Just consider the sheer number of differences in education, skill levels, culture, and expectations between the Japanese and North Americans. But quite a few Japanese companies, including several large automakers, have been remarkably effective at creating some of the highest-quality, most productive work forces in North America. They've done so by taking a systematic and thorough approach to making employment decisions that puts most U.S. and Canadian companies to shame. Unfortunately, these success stories with production workers and supervisors are rarely duplicated with North American managers and professionals. Before we examine why, it might be useful to review some of the features that can make the Japanese selection systems so successful at the employee level.

Japanese operations in North America that have hired successfully have started with a thorough understanding of the "dimensions" (behaviors, motivations, and knowledge) required of each job category in the organization (see box below). Typically, after these dimensions are identified, a comprehensive selection system is developed that evaluates applicants on each dimension. Paper-and-pencil instruments are used to evaluate some dimensions; interviews

---

WHAT A GROUP LEADER NEEDS

The following is a list of dimensions used by one Japanese company for a group leader or supervisor position:

GROUP LEADER DIMENSIONS

Analysis (Problem Identification)
Business Planning
Collaboration
Communication (Oral and Written)
Delegation of Authority and Responsibility/Follow-up
Developing Organizational Talent
Individual Leadership (Influence)
Information Monitoring
Initiative
Judgment (Problem Solution)
Maximizing Performance
Meeting Leadership
Motivation to Empower Others
Operational Planning
Organizational Fit (Compatibility of Personal Values with Values of the Organization)
Rapport Building
Work Standards

are used for others. However, a unique aspect of the selection systems applied by Japanese organizations is the use of behavioral simulations.

Behavioral simulations provide opportunities to see an applicant in action. For example, an applicant might be given information on a quality problem in a hypothetical manufacturing situation. After studying the information, the applicant is given the opportunity to seek additional information by questioning a resource person. The applicant's challenge is to pin down the causes of the problem and suggest a solution. Here, analysis and decision-making skills are evaluated. In another exercise, a group of applicants might be formed into a team and challenged to find solutions to several team-related problems. In this instance, team participation, analysis, and leadership skills are evaluated. Many manufacturing organizations simulate a major component of the job to assess an applicant's ability to learn a task, work at a defined pace, and make improvement recommendations *(kaizen)*. Toyota, for example, used two such simulations, each lasting three hours, in staffing its Georgetown, Kentucky, plant.

EXAMPLE OF A DIMENSION DEFINITION

Each dimension is defined and numerous examples are given for why the dimension is important on the job. The following is an example of how one dimension is defined, along with key indicators of performance for the dimension. Representative examples of performance are also shown.

Delegation/Follow-up: Allocating decision-making authority and task responsibilities to appropriate subordinates; utilizing subordinates' time, skills, and potential effectively; establishing procedures to monitor the results of delegations, assignments, or project contingencies.

KEY INDICATORS

1. Task delegated—Assignment of responsibility for action/ authority to make decisions.
2. Target of delegation—Assignment to the appropriate person based on organizational correctness, the knowledge/skills of the

continued

individual, and opportunity for the development of individual skills.

3. Clarity of delegation—Description of actions required, constraints on actions, and deadlines; description of problems anticipated and resources suggested.

4. Coaching or help offered—Mutual determination of problem areas and the offer of assistance.

5. Persuasiveness of delegation—Convincing statement of the purpose and importance of the action.

6. Feedback—Means and due date for reporting the results of the assigned or delegated tasks.

REPRESENTATIVE EXAMPLES FROM THE JOB ANALYSES

1. Schedule and assign employees to multiple activities; monitor progress; reassign employees to maintain efficiency and timeliness.

2. Explain the importance of assignments and completion dates to the employees executing them.

3. Consider employees' interests, strengths, and development needs in assigning tasks.

4. Delegate problem-solving and decision-making responsibilities to employees. (For example, allow employees to determine the action that needs to be taken when a part is not immediately available.)

5. Ensure that employees have what they need to succeed on delegated assignments; assess roadblocks to completing assignments independently (such as lack of materials, guidance, authority, or skills).

6. Use techniques/technologies such as personal computers to monitor productivity and performance; stay informed of the status of projects/jobs; and track future work load.

7. Monitor performance by observing employees directly and by using system techniques such as indices.

Not all applicants go through all of these selection exercises. Jobs in Japanese organizations are often highly coveted by North Americans, especially in regions with low wages and high unemployment. It is not uncommon for as many as ten individuals to apply for every one open position. The selection system is set up as a series of screens. Each screen eliminates successively more applicants until the most qualified are identified. Because behavioral simulations can be time-consuming, they are used with the handful who emerge as the best candidates. Figure 13.1 shows a sample selection system and the percentage of candidates remaining in the system at each stage.

FIGURE 13.1
SAMPLE MANUFACTURING EMPLOYEE SELECTION SYSTEM

	Percentage Remaining in System at Completion of Phase
Phase 1: Advertising and Recruitment	100
Phase 2: Orientation and Application	
A. Video job orientation	
B. Application	
(Self-selection out of the system)	90
Phase 3: Initial Screening	
A. Screening interview	
B. Cognitive ability test	
C. Motivational inventory	40
Phase 4: Assessment Center Exercises	
A. Group problem-solving exercise	
B. Individual problem-solving exercise	
C. Manufacturing exercise	
D. One-on-one interaction exercise	20
Phase 5: Final Screening	
A. Reference checks	
B. Targeted interviews	12
Phase 6: Job Offer	11
Phase 7: Health Assessment	
A. Drug and alcohol test	
B. Physical exam	10

This process represents a substantial investment of time and money for Japanese organizations. The investment is far greater than that made by typical North American companies. Why go to such elaborate lengths? For many Japanese organizations, the answer is simple: Their production systems depend on flexible, motivated, high-quality employees. It's impossible to find employees of that quality when you take a casual approach to hiring, especially considering the diversity of U.S. and Canadian workers in areas such as analytical problem-solving skills, interpersonal skills, and job motivation. Almost all Japanese high school or college graduates might possess acceptable levels of these skills and motivations, but such an assumption is dangerous in North America. Because Japanese production systems leave little room for unproductive employees, it's vital to make sure that only the best employees are hired.

Concerns about U.S. and Canadian employment laws also motivate Japanese companies to use these more advanced selection systems. These laws require specific selection practices to assure equal treatment of minorities, women, and other groups. Because many Japanese companies are concerned about their community image in North America, they make great efforts to appear to be model employers, starting with scrupulously fair hiring practices.

An informal survey of twelve Japanese companies that have used such comprehensive selection systems and methodologies, including behavioral simulations, indicates that such efforts appear to be working. All twelve companies report high levels of satisfaction with the quality of their employees, team leaders, and group leaders. For example, Toyota reports little employee turnover and few employment-related problems. Moreover, in a relatively short period of time, the company says the quality of the cars it produces in Kentucky equals the quality of those produced in Japan.

Not all Japanese companies can make similar claims. Like many North American companies, some Japanese companies in North America hire with little thought to job skills or motivation. Our experience suggests that Japanese companies seem to suffer more from this oversight than North American companies in the same industries and geographical areas. Turnover can be very high in Japanese companies with casual hiring practices. We've watched one Japanese company endure a 30-percent annual turnover rate. Japanese managers at this company are frustrated by the poor productivity of their North American employees, which makes the managers look very bad to their superiors in Tokyo. The managers tend to blame the poor work ethic of the local population. Instead, they probably should blame the fact that they hired the wrong kind of employees.

PROBLEMS WITH MANAGERS

The same Japanese companies that are pleased with the productivity and motivation of their carefully selected North American employees and supervisors are often disappointed by their North American managers and executives, whom they find lacking in analytical and people skills. Moreover, Japanese companies often are confused by the adjustment problems of North American managers and executives in Japanese organizations. They just don't seem to fit in. Part of the problem is that few Japanese organizations have paid attention to the problem of what fitting in means to a North American manager.

An American human resources consultant who has worked for several Japanese companies says:

> Most Japanese companies haven't done a good job at all with their managers and executives. They have these bright, creative people in the lower levels of the organization, but the middle level—the managers brought in from American companies—are weak in the Japanese sense. At the lower levels, they've got people selected for the environment because the environment has been well-defined. But the environment for American managers has been barely defined at all. Just what are they supposed to do? What are their limits and potential? How much control and responsibility are they supposed to have? It's a real muddle.

Several factors contribute to the muddle. North American managers in Japanese firms often are selected with the aid of executive recruiters (or "headhunters") who focus more on a candidate's technical skills and past experience in North American companies than on cultural sensitivity and adaptability. Japanese interviewers, often lacking interviewing skills (see next chapter), frequently rely on a gut feeling and personal chemistry, leading to evaluations of candidates that are cursory at best. And while management positions are much more complicated and critical to the organization's success than lower-level positions, behavioral simulations, tests, or other more sophisticated methodologies are rarely used. As a result, Japanese organizations might spend more time scrutinizing the suitability of an average North American production worker than they do a North American senior manager or even vice-president.

Japanese organizations offer various reasons for their lack of attention to managerial hiring. Some Japanese executives say that they assume people coming from important North American organizations will have adequate skills. Therefore, checking or testing for those skills, which would probably deeply insult a candidate anyway, is unnecessary. Others say they are too rushed in starting up new operations to give selection full attention. Still others believe that executive recruiters evaluate the candidates more than they actually do.

THE SELECTION PROCESS

Organizational fit refers to the compatibility of an individual with an organization's style of operation and values. If the needs that drive an individual and the ability of an organization to meet those needs don't match, the gap will eventually result in the dissatisfaction of the individual. What kind of North American manager finds satisfaction in Japanese organizations? The study by Egon Zehnder, referred to earlier, concluded that satisfied and effective local managers are "flexible and highly tolerant of ambiguity."

In a constellation of characteristics the authors called "patient aggressiveness," North American managers who reported they worked well in Japanese organizations didn't need a clear chain of command and well-defined rules and procedures to operate, and they had the patience to listen and communicate clearly.* They weren't exactly nonassertive, but they preferred to take a low-key, nonconfrontational approach to managing—a style marked by politeness and civility, rather than loud demands and "table pounding." They could swallow their pride and enthusiastically implement decisions in which

---

* *Management Culture and the Effectiveness of Local Executives in Japanese-Owned U.S. Corporations.* Egon Zehnder International, Tokyo/The University of Michigan, 1990, p. 79.

they played no part, preserving harmony by stifling any sign of personal disagreement when they saw that a decision was inevitable.

Unfortunately, the ability of Japanese companies to find such people is often more a matter of luck than design. A primary reason for this difficulty may be the way managers are hired in Japan, which proves a poor model for hiring in North America. With few exceptions, large companies in Japan do not select managers from outside the organization. They promote from within, using years of performance data in a variety of positions to make their decisions. Very often it is the personnel department that makes the promotion decision, not Japanese line managers. It's no wonder, then, that Japanese organizations have difficulty adjusting to hiring managers in North America. They simply are inexperienced.

Of course, there have been notable examples of Japanese organizations hiring outstanding North American executives. To experience more success stories, Japanese organizations must apply the same sophisticated selection technology at the managerial and executive levels that they now apply at the employee level. For example, several Japanese companies are putting manager applicants through simulations that depict everyday job situations in Japanese-owned organizations.

REALISTIC JOB PREVIEWS

Many progressive Japanese companies are deeply concerned that new employees understand how very different their new jobs will be from jobs in typical North American companies. That's why Toyota, Subaru-Isuzu Automotive, Inc. (SIA), and CAMI (a joint venture between General Motors and Suzuki), among many others, have developed orientation videos that give applicants a fairly complete picture of life as a team member or group leader. These videos realistically depict the pace and pressure of the work environment and the values of the organization—values that applicants will be expected to share if they're hired.

Subaru-Isuzu's video, for example, tells applicants that employees are expected to share values such as teamwork and cooperation; a commitment to quality, *kaizen*, eliminating waste, and safety; and a

continued

willingness to develop and use multiple skills. The message, illustrated in various ways, is that applicants who can't develop a commitment to these values need go no further in the application process.

The orientation videos also familiarize applicants with the assessment exercises they will encounter as part of the hiring process. This is important, since the length and complexity of the selection process can come as a shock to many North Americans. The videos explain that one reason for all the tests and simulations is the fact that Japanese companies believe it is essential to hire only those who have the ability to be successful in the organization.

Upward of 20 percent of applicants might decide not to continue the selection process after seeing these orientation videos. In this sense alone, the videos deliver a handsome return on their production costs by helping companies avoid the expense of processing applicants who would eventually be found to be ill-suited for the open positions.

The assessment process itself is another method of providing a realistic job preview. For example, if a simulated production process is used, applicants get a sense for the pace of production required by the organization, and for the lifting and manipulation of objects required by various production jobs. Perhaps even more important, they discover what it will be like to work in teams to solve problems—a key feature of many Japanese production systems and often the one most unfamiliar to North Americans.

Extensive behavioral interviews make up the last stage of most selection systems for team members, leaders, and group leaders. Trained interviewers focus on motivation and job fit by exploring with applicants the things they have enjoyed in past jobs, and then comparing those features with those that are available in the new job. Interviewers also check the reality of an applicant's expectations. Some applicants complete the entire selection process and still don't fully appreciate what the job will be like or understand the need for teamwork and continuous improvement. Thus, the interviewer's "reality check" is an important step in the overall process. Applicants who complete the entire selection process and are eventually hired are seldom surprised or disappointed by what they encounter on the job. After all, they were selected for their ability to fit in.

During these simulations many potential indicators of success are assessed, including the ability of North American applicants to communicate in a multicultural environment, to work effectively with a coordinator or advisor, to reach consensus-based, collaborative decisions, to learn Japanese production and management methods, and more. Organizations are assured of individuals with a broader range of competencies, rather than competencies limited to a few technical areas, or competencies that are inappropriate in Japanese organizations. In turn, applicants gain a clear understanding of how satisfying they might find life in a Japanese company. If they later feel disappointed, both they and their Japanese employer share the responsibility. The Japanese organizations with the most sophisticated managerial selection systems often have developed them upon opening their second North American operation or when a plant added a second shift. As lessons are learned from early mistakes, more sophisticated selection technology is adopted in staffing new operations.

Luckily, the technology required to improve the accuracy of selecting middle- and higher-level managers is available and well tested. The process might involve a combination of paper-and-pencil tests, behavioral simulations, and several "targeted" interviews (see Chapter 14). Outside consultants may aid in the evaluations, but it is important that the responsibility for the final decision rests fully with the hiring organization.

Arguably, a significant number of the middle-management problems outlined in this book could be solved through better selection of North American middle managers. At the very least, a comprehensive job analysis should be completed for each managerial position. A job analysis provides the basis for an accurate and legally defensible selection system. At the same time, it provides the applicant with a better understanding of the kind of position he or she will fill in the organization.

Furthermore, we recommend that Japanese firms spend more time in accurately describing positions to applicants. These descriptions must be realistic, particularly in terms of the decision-making and career opportunities available to applicants. Japanese companies in North America tend to oversell how "American" they've become, or at least are committed to becoming. Thus, when their uniquely Japanese characteristics become apparent, local managers might feel the organization isn't living up to its word. Opportunities do exist in Japanese firms for the right kind of North American manager. To seize those opportunities, many potential North American management candidates will gladly modify other expectations. But if some personal trade-off is required, candidates must have the chance to make that decision before they are hired.

14

INTERVIEWING NORTH AMERICANS

(To the Japanese), every single job applicant who walked through the door was a surprise.

AMERICAN MANAGER

INTERVIEWS PLAY DIFFERENT roles in the job-selection process in Japanese and North American organizations. In Japanese organizations, job interviews are often a formality. In North American organizations, interviews usually play a key role in finding the right people for important positions. As a consequence, training managers to interview effectively is important to North American organizations, whereas Japanese managers might receive little, if any, interviewing training. Because conducting interviews properly has legal implications in North America, organizations might spend additional time and money ensuring that interviewers are up-to-date on employment laws. That's not as simple as it sounds because employment law is continuously evolving in the United States and Canada.

The degree of importance placed on interviews and the relative inexperience of Japanese managers in interviewing North Americans has several consequences. For one, Japanese managers often impress

North Americans as insensitive to the nuances of interviewing job applicants. They make blunders few North Americans would make. And they often want to hire people who seem all wrong to North Americans.

Another consequence is often tied to the limited English skills of many Japanese managers. It is extremely difficult to extract meaningful information from North American applicants when basic communication itself is such a challenge. Sometimes the language barrier is so great that Japanese managers virtually remove themselves from the selection process, relying instead on North American managers to recruit, interview, and hire. North American managers say they often battle this tendency because the participation of Japanese managers in interviewing is essential if a "blended" organization is to be achieved. At the very least, says one American manager, "It conveys some of the reality of communication challenges within the organization. The sooner people find out about this, the better."

The poor English skills of some Japanese managers also make them reluctant to probe applicants for fear of seeming rude or causing loss of face. Frequently, a North American manager will do all the talking while Japanese managers silently observe. Sometimes, to the consternation of applicants, Japanese managers might even slip into a contemplative state that mimics sleeping. "I got a little worried," an American manager recalls. "When you're putting people to sleep whom you're trying to impress, it's probably not a good sign."

OFF-LIMITS

Many Japanese managers participating in the hiring process say they received some training in Japan on the very different legal regulations in the United States and Canada that make the simple process of hiring a person seem maddeningly complex. Even so, North American managers are often surprised by the tendency of their Japanese colleagues to stumble into areas regarding an applicant's personal life and beliefs that most North Americans would consider off-limits. "They do a lot of little things that put them on the spot when they evaluate new people. Not intentionally, but they just don't realize how disturbing some of these things can be to Americans," observes an American manager in a joint venture with a Japanese company.

> When we were hiring, it was surprising how many people they found objectionable—fellows without hair and fellows with round tummies, fellows who had been divorced or ones who weren't married. They looked to see how old someone was, how skinny or fat they were, since if people don't have enough respect to take care of their bodies, it says something about them. They would ask people about eating, exercise, religion. Some Japanese managers would ask rather pointed questions in some very personal areas. You have to stop them because their questions are often illegal.

This same manager says his joint venture developed clear policies on the hiring process but that Japanese managers found them easy to ignore—not so much out of indifference to the sensitivity of applicants and the requirements of U.S. law but more because it was "a cultural shock to them to be interviewing some of the people we interviewed." In Japan, these managers were used to seeing job applicants fresh out of college and never before had evaluated middle-aged applicants or minorities or women. In most of North America, job applicants from all three of these groups are common. "Every single job applicant who walked through the door was a surprise," the American says. "And they fell back on this line of questioning that made it sound more like the person in the chair in front of them was asking for their daughter's hand in marriage instead of some supervisory job on the plant floor."

SUPERFICIAL QUALITIES

An exercise in the "Access to Success" Overseas Manager Program, run by the Management Services Center in Japan, illustrates the contrast between Japanese and North American approaches to evaluating job applicants. The program is designed to help Japanese managers develop skills needed to succeed in North America and other parts of the world. Part of the program consists of watching videotapes of three simulated interviews for the same sales job.

Actors portray the job applicants. Based on what participants in the program have been told about the job requirements and the qualities needed for someone to fit smoothly into the organization, their task is to evaluate responses to questions and determine what more they need to know to select the applicant with the greatest chance of success.

The first applicant, a young black man, appears clearly qualified, although his personal history is more complicated than the other two (twice divorced, single parent). He appears a little nervous and is almost excessively modest, but as he describes his previous work experiences in detail, it becomes clear that he has the potential to do a very good job as a salesperson. He cites many instances of working closely with customers to solve problems and cement lasting relationships. He appears to be a tireless worker, thrives on "solution" selling, and seems instinctively attuned to customer needs and satisfaction.

The second applicant, a somewhat older woman, also can cite past successes, including one $40-million sale. But as the interview progresses and she provides details about her past work experiences, it becomes clear that her strengths lie in the analysis and organization of large, complex sales, not in actual selling. She lacks the people skills and the motivation to be effective in a day-to-day sales position, where routine sales are the rule. She might be useful to the company in some fashion, but not in the open sales position.

The third applicant starts out spectacularly. Blond, athletic, and smooth talking, he seems to know all the right words and all the right ways to flatter the interviewer. After a series of questions, however, a different picture begins to emerge, at least to experienced North American interviewers. It becomes clear from the applicant's descriptions of previous work experiences that he relied on luck and selling to friends and family connections to generate business. There are alarming gaps in his past work history and, as he tries to gloss over them, he can't quite disguise the fact that his work experiences were characterized by inattention to detail and customer needs and sheer laziness. He closed more deals on the golf course and at the country club than through hard work and creative selling. What he has going for him are his good looks and unwavering eye contact, his smile, and his well-rehearsed pitch that manages to say nothing, but somehow does it with style.

Younger Japanese managers with good English skills but no training in interviewing often conclude that the smooth-talking third candidate is the best of the three. Younger Japanese managers with poor English skills often pick the female candidate. Both candidates are wrong for the job, but they excel at selling themselves and are attractive as well. Most North American managers quickly notice their flaws and far less frequently make the same mistakes, choosing instead the first candidate, who lacks the cosmetic qualities of the other two candidates but is clearly right for the job.

The mistake Japanese managers make in the exercise often repeats itself in real-life job interviews. Unfamiliar with the great diversity of backgrounds and experiences—and forced for the first time to interview blacks, Hispanics, and women—some Japanese managers focus on superficial qualities instead of more meaningful criteria. Interviewing is not necessarily something North American managers are good at either, but as cultural "insiders" they have an easier time separating superficial qualities from qualities that are relevant to the demands of the job.

WHAT CAN YOU ASK?

Japanese managers attempting to become effective interviewers in North America often become frustrated by what they perceive as the overpowering constraints imposed by Equal Employment Opportunity laws. The training Japanese managers receive seems to be focused on what they *can't* ask because of legal restrictions, rather than on how they *can* interview effectively.

We believe strongly that the best way to train interviewers is to train them on what they can do, not on what they cannot do. If an interviewer has a firm understanding of the dimensions associated with success on a particular job and has the skill to seek behaviors, knowledge, or motivations related to those dimensions, and only those dimensions, the interviewer doesn't have to worry about illegal questions. Truly job-related questions are legal. Many Japanese managers in the United States have been successfully trained in conducting effective, targeted interviews. They appreciate the precision and rigor of an organized, data-based selection program, and they quickly develop the skill and the confidence to conduct effective, legally defensible interviews.

QUESTIONS *NOT* TO ASK IN AN INTERVIEW

Various national, state, and local laws prohibit certain questions as part of the selection process unless bona fide occupational requirements can be proven. Prohibited areas of questioning include:

- Age (if the applicant is forty years of age or older; in Massachusetts, under eighteen)
- Race
- National origin (except to determine legal residency in the United States)
- Religion
- Marital status (married, single, divorced, engaged, living with someone)
- Number of dependents
- Child care
- Housing (own home, rent, live with parents)
- Arrest record
- Health status
- Type of discharge from military
- Willingness to work weekends (unless inability to assign the person to such work would cause "chaotic personnel problems")
- Any information from minority or female applicants not routinely requested of white or male applicants

Federal law prohibits direct questions or questions that might imply discriminatory bias. "Are you a member of the Golden Agers?" or "Is St. Helen's a parochial school?" are examples of prohibited questions.

COMMON MISTAKES MADE BY *BOTH* NORTH AMERICAN AND JAPANESE MANAGERS DURING THE HIRING PROCESS

- **Interviewers fail to get information from applicants on all the dimensions (competencies or performance requirements) needed to be successful in the job.** Usually, they attempt to get information on

continued

only a few dimensions they believe to be the most important or the easiest to evaluate, ignoring other dimensions that might affect performance.

• **Interviewers permit one dimension—favorable or unfavorable—to influence their judgment on other dimensions.** This is often called the "halo effect." One outstanding accomplishment or dimension becomes a "halo" that obscures other, less attractive dimensions. The halo also can affect judgments in the opposite direction. An applicant's weakness or limitations in some areas, which might possibly be improved by training, obscure the applicant's strengths.

• **Interviewers overlap in their coverage of some dimensions.** Often when several people interview an applicant, they ask the same questions. Ultimately, decisions must be made based on limited or redundant information.

• **Interviewers misinterpret applicant information.** In the more volatile and heterogeneous North American employment market, the best predictor of future performance is past performance—not guesses about future potential. However, many interviewers ask applicants what they *would* do in a given situation, instead of what they *have done* in previous jobs. This focus on theoretical information forces interviewers to interpret the meaning of the applicant's responses, an approach prone to misjudgments and mistakes. This approach also allows interviewers to be fooled by an applicant's "selling" skills (like those used by the third applicant in the Overseas Manager Program videotapes).

• **Interviewers ignore job motivation.** Job motivation is different from general motivation. A person might be highly motivated to do many things, but not by the factors associated with a specific job. In any organization, an outstanding engineer who enjoys solving technical problems might not find much satisfaction as a manager with little hands-on project work. In a Japanese organization, a strong-willed manager might be extremely motivated to manage in a relatively autonomous fashion but frustrated in a position that requires reliance on consensus decision making and tutelage by coordinators and advisors.

continued

• **Interviewers ignore organizational fit.** As we've suggested, determining organizational fit is particularly difficult in a North American-based Japanese organization. To start with, it requires attention to how North American managers are supposed to fit in, what development opportunities the organization intends to give them to keep their contributions to the company growing and their personal satisfaction high, and the organization's guiding values. Then the compatibility of the applicant's needs to these factors must be evaluated. The performance of even the most qualified manager eventually will suffer if the organizational fit is bad.

• **Interviewers' judgments can be affected by biases and stereotypes.** Without a systematic approach to evaluating applicants, interviewers fall back on an applicant's personal qualities that have nothing to do with how well he or she might perform the job. Many Japanese managers in North America admit to having little exposure to people outside their own (very narrow) work and social groups in Japan. This could be a primary reason why North American managers say their Japanese colleagues seem especially likely to fall prey to this syndrome.

• **Interviewers allow applicants to control the interview.** Interviewers who allow applicants to talk about anything they want usually get a lot of words but little information about past jobs and job-related experiences. Chance plays a big role; the applicant might or might not provide information related to job success. Effective interviewers systematically direct the interview into areas that will yield job-related information.

• **Applicants are "turned off" by the interviewing process.** Many North Americans view the chance to work for a Japanese company positively, but they are turned off by the interview process. For one thing, the silent presence of Japanese managers during interviews can be confusing. "It was a little strange," one American manager recalls of her interview with a Southern California subsidiary of a major Japanese bank. "One American did all the talking, and three Japanese gentlemen sat there silently, occasionally talking among themselves." Later, after being hired, she learned that it wasn't that the Japanese managers weren't interested in her and her qualifications;

continued

they were just reluctant to question her directly out of embarrassment over their own limited English skills and a fear of being misunderstood.

• Interviewers don't systematically integrate data before making final decisions. Whether two or three managers interview applicants separately, or whether managers together interview applicants, there is a need to systematically review the data obtained before making a final decision about the applicant. This review and decision making should be built around the job-related dimensions defined as important to job success. If an organization does not evaluate the candidate against each job-related dimension before making a selection decision, it is very likely that mistakes will be made because important dimensions will be overlooked. One of the surest ways to overcome the "halo effect" is to force managers to evaluate candidates against a comprehensive list of job-related dimensions. This approach minimizes the tendency to be influenced by a few very positive qualities and forces the organization to look at the entire person.

15

MANAGING OR MISMANAGING DIVERSITY:

JAPANESE ORGANIZATIONS AND THE EEO CHALLENGE

When we told our [Japanese] production advisor that we wanted to send a female team leader to Japan for training, he really lost his composure. "What about the bathrooms?" he asked. "Will she have as much stamina as men?" "Can a woman really understand how hard it will be?" "How could she possibly be qualified?" "Didn't we understand the confusing and demoralizing effects this would have on the other employees?" And on and on and on.

Well, we insisted, and she went. She was the first woman in this production area the company had ever seen. She stood her ground, which wasn't easy, was highly competent (we knew she would be), and was such a novelty that she ended up as a kind of celebrity. Japanese managers would bring others in just to see her. Newspapers came in and took her picture. They ended up just going wild over her. She came back here feeling like a queen. It's amazing how old-fashioned they are about women who don't fit the stereotype of the women who come in and help out and then "retire" when they get married.

AMERICAN MANAGER

172

COSTLY MISTAKES

ONE OF THE GREATEST challenges of operating any facility in the United States or Canada is the increasingly comprehensive web of laws and regulations designed to prohibit hiring and other employment practices based on "non-job-related" factors. Those factors today include race, gender, origin of birth, disability, and age. Individuals who feel their rights have been violated by an employer can hire an attorney and file a lawsuit. Every year tens of thousands of North Americans do just that.

Some Japanese organizations have modeled sound hiring practices by recruiting work forces that accurately reflect the demographics of surrounding communities, particularly with regard to blacks and other minority groups. The National Urban League, a U.S. organization that promotes, among other things, minority employment, gave Toyota a special recognition award for its hiring record at its Georgetown, Kentucky, automotive assembly plant. Toyota's Georgetown operation and other Japanese companies have demonstrated that work forces that meet Japanese standards for quality and productivity and reflect local demographics can be hired while meeting all the legal requirements of various government agencies.

Other Japanese organizations aren't faring nearly as well. According to various court rulings, including a 1982 ruling by the U.S. Supreme Court, Japanese subsidiaries are subject to the same local employment laws as North American organizations. But that hasn't prevented many Japanese companies from making costly mistakes. To North American managers, Japanese managers often seem poorly trained when it comes to employment practices in North America. And few Japanese managers can rely on experience since the employment situations in North America and Japan are profoundly different. Many observers, including North Americans employed by Japanese companies, have noted a defiant "go ahead and sue" attitude toward employment regulations by some Japanese companies in North America.

Some experts predict that the nineties will see many Japanese companies bogged down in an endless series of legal battles. These observers feel the "honeymoon" between Japanese employers and local workers is over and that Equal Employment Opportunity Commission (EEOC)* problems, which have been years in the making, will start erupting. Penalties in such instances can be substantial, with individuals and/or groups awarded years of back pay and other damages. Honda Motors lost a job discrimination suit, for example, and was ordered to pay "lost wages" to 370 people in Ohio who were turned down for jobs several years earlier. The cost to the company was $6 million.† But court awards are only the tip of the iceberg. Tens of millions of dollars more are spent by Japanese companies each year in out-of-court settlements. The figure is much higher if you include the hundreds of millions of dollars spent on legal fees.

Japanese companies are coming under increased scrutiny in North America. Fair or not, many are perceived to favor white males over qualified minorities and women. This reputation poses more than just an image problem. Because it can discourage minority and female applicants, Japanese companies often must make extraordinary efforts to recruit qualified applicants. And because they often are watched closely by minority rights advocacy groups, Japanese companies must be extremely vigilant in assuring that their selection/promotion systems and personnel practices can withstand legal challenges.

NEW FRONTIERS, NEW PITFALLS

The challenge of fair employment practices in North America goes beyond gender and race discrimination, although those two charges often draw the most attention. Age discrimination, a fairly new frontier in the evolving definition of fair employment practices in North America, represents another troublesome area for Japanese companies. In one recent case, a major Japanese electronics manufacturer lost a multi-million-dollar suit after a jury in Illinois ruled that the company discriminated against a middle-aged job applicant.‡ During the trial, various U.S. experts described a Japanese "system" that

---

* The Equal Employment Opportunity Commission is the umbrella enforcement authority for a series of U.S. federal employment practices mandates.

† "Working with the Japanese 101." *Business Tokyo*, October 1990, p. 40.

‡ Kilbourn, P. T. "U.S. Managers Claim Job Bias by the Japanese." *New York Times*, June 1, 1990.

virtually precluded hiring middle-aged people from outside the company for management positions and forcibly retired employees at age fifty-five. Both practices might be acceptable in Japan, the jury concluded, but they are discriminatory in the United States.

Other aspects of the Japanese "system" pose problems for Japanese companies in North America. Physical handicaps and factors such as weight, height, appearance, and the way applicants seem to care for their health are not legal reasons for denying employment in the United States and Canada. Various laws require that physical appearance be ignored in making hiring decisions. More recently, the U.S. Congress passed the Americans with Disabilities Act (ADA), which requires that reasonable accommodations be made for the handicapped.

Equal Employment Opportunity concerns pose a tremendous challenge to Japanese ideas about staffing and operating facilities. They could force Japanese organizations in North America to reshape themselves to a certain extent. Recently, one of the largest Japanese trading companies settled a lawsuit that accused its U.S. subsidiary of, among other things, closing its upper-management ranks to non-Japanese. At issue was the very basic practice of rotating Japanese personnel from Tokyo headquarters through senior positions in the United States, instead of promoting local employees. This practice, the plaintiffs argued, was discriminatory. A U.S. federal court agreed. Under the terms of the court agreement, the company must make "good faith" efforts to increase the number of U.S. executives in senior positions and develop career development programs to give local managers a better chance of moving into top-management jobs. These efforts include rotating local managers back to Japan, a dramatic change for the company. The plaintiffs' attorney pointed out to the U.S. press that other Japanese companies practice the same policy and warned that more suits will follow.*

Similar allegations of the "anti-American" bias of Japanese companies surface when Japanese operations lay off employees. Invariably, local employees lose their jobs while Japanese employees are reassigned. For many, it provides further evidence that Japanese companies discriminate against non-Japanese. This perception might

---

* Jacobs, D. L. "Japanese American Cultural Clash." *New York Times,* September 1, 1990.

not disappear completely until Japanese companies are able to assign and promote non-Japanese employees in the same manner as they do Japanese managers. (See Chapter 16.)

A ROLE FOR WOMEN IN JAPANESE ORGANIZATIONS?

Women have a long and difficult history of trying to stake out roles in North American businesses. In recent years, they've made astonishing progress, although women have yet to really crack the upper echelons of North American business. Today, 37 percent of managers in the United States are women, according to U.S. government figures. The figure continues to rise steadily. The comparable figure in Japan is 2 percent. Thus, the rarity of female managers in Japan helps account for some of the sheer "strangeness" women managers in North America feel working with male Japanese colleagues and the widespread belief that Japanese organizations are simply unsympathetic to competent, professional women.

"The patronizing, condescension, suspiciousness—it's like where the American companies I've worked for were twenty years ago," says an American woman with a Japanese bank in New York City. "You have to get used to things you forgot existed." The number of highly qualified North American women who report that Japanese managers refuse to take them "seriously" is too great to ignore. Many North American women report that Japanese managers interfere in their roles as managers and their relationships with subordinates. For example, Japanese managers might step in and "help" a female manager with problems that they'd encourage male employees to handle on their own. North American women also say Japanese managers go over their heads and deal directly with their male superiors when the matter should have been discussed with them.

Even when women are promoted to the manager level, subtle pressures to perform menial or clerical jobs persist. When they don't act suitably subservient, many women say, they risk being perceived as "threatening" to male Japanese managers, who retaliate by being excessively critical. "I've been told by my Japanese colleagues that they disapprove of the way I stand, the way I walk, the fact that I have a can of soda on my desk," says one woman. "These are things they wouldn't dare say to males."

Female trainees in Japanese organizations sometimes have an especially difficult time. "The notion that we're here to begin with boggles the minds of Japanese trainers, and the notion that we could ever become as skilled and productive as males is something they don't even want to consider," a woman recalls of her training days at a Japanese manufacturing facility in the South. At that facility, Japanese trainers initially refused to acknowledge questions from female trainees, who were essentially treated as if they were invisible. When the trainers were disciplined by Japanese managers (only after several women contacted lawyers), the trainers at last acknowledged the female trainees, but usually only to react sarcastically to their questions. The battle, which continues, will probably be resolved in court.

"Old habits die hard," says a male American manager at another Japanese manufacturing facility:

> Our Japanese trainers here are often old enough to be the fathers of the women they train. Their daughters would never think of a career such as these women are contemplating. And they certainly wouldn't be working alongside men in such a male-dominated business. Despite the training the trainers received in Japan on the differences between Japanese and American women, they just can't convince themselves that this is an appropriate thing for women to do, and hard as they try, it inevitably shows up in their behavior.

Japanese-American women who speak Japanese and understand Japanese culture may encounter even greater difficulties in Japanese organizations. While many Japanese managers have learned to accept, or at least tolerate, North American women, when these same managers see a Japanese or Oriental face—even if the woman is a third-generation American—they revert to practices that might not seem out of place in Japan but are definitely inappropriate in North America. One Japanese executive is reported to have insisted that his Japanese-American secretary kneel while serving tea. Others have asked their Japanese-American secretaries to walk behind them in humiliating displays of obsequiousness. Says one Japanese-American woman:

> If American women are treated as second-class citizens in Japanese companies, then non-Japanese Oriental women are third class, and

women with Japanese ancestry are fourth class. I get tired of being the one asked to stay late or come in early. Apparently they don't think anything of asking me to do something extra, but they are reluctant to ask my American colleagues.

The New Reality

Organized women's groups in the United States are especially suspicious of Japanese organizations. This is not surprising considering that many of the discrimination suits against Japanese organizations in recent years have involved sex discrimination. Plaintiffs in these suits say they were denied opportunities for advancement and were offered less pay than men for the same jobs. The reason: Japanese employers seem to believe that women will inevitably quit to marry and raise families. Therefore, they represent less potential value to the organization than male employees.

That attitude collides head-on with the new realities of the North American workplace. An increasing number of North American women are seeking long-term careers. Many are heads of households who have no choice but to work. The male dominance of North American business is steadily being chipped away as women prove their ability in all types of jobs at all levels. Today, most North American executives are accustomed to working with women and no longer give it a second thought. In blue-collar jobs and professions the situation is similar. Gender bias is still a reality, but changing attitudes and legal sanctions have sex discrimination under siege.

Demographics play a big role in these changing attitudes. White males have become a minority among new entrants into the North American labor pool. To many North American companies, it has become clear that meeting labor needs will require recruiting and hiring women and minorities for all positions. These same companies also have made rapid progress in developing human resources programs and management policies that consider the special needs of diverse groups of employees.

Many Japanese companies have done an exemplary job of adapting work to the special needs of women and minorities at the employee level. Far fewer have made attempts to make female managers feel at home. These Japanese companies seem uncharacteristically shortsighted. A reputation of unfairness to female managers and a lack of opportunities will eliminate a great source of qualified applicants. The Japanese attitude toward working women might be another area in which Japanese companies put themselves at an unnecessary competitive disadvantage in North America.

What needs to be done? Attitudes toward working women in Japan are changing significantly. Women are working longer, returning to the workplace after having children, and gaining increased respect for their professional competence and achievements. Also, younger Japanese male managers are less affected by traditional Japanese stereotypes of working women. These changes lead us to think that unequal treatment of women in Japanese organizations in North America will diminish over time. But Japanese companies must take a more aggressive approach. They can't afford to let time alone solve the problem.

Japanese organizations need to adopt new and more creative ways to make Japanese managers more sensitive to women in the workplace in North America. The threat of legal action is ineffective in prompting change. More extensive training is needed—with a concentration on behavioral change, not cognitive understanding. Training programs that provide opportunities to practice the key principles (see Chapters 9 and 10) should use situations in which a manager must deal with a female employee. In this way, the Japanese will learn to use the key principles in general and with women specifically. Clearly, Japanese organizations must make conscious and substantial efforts to ensure equal treatment for all employees. Affirmative action in the hiring, promotion, and treatment of women must be the norm, and actions to ensure equal treatment must be reinforced by higher management.

PART FOUR

SHARED RESPONSIBILITY FOR DEVELOPING INDIVIDUALS AND THE ORGANIZATION

16

DEVELOPING TALENT WITH TRAINING

Americans think training is the answer to everything. In reality, discipline, enthusiasm, experience—not hours spent in a classroom—are usually required to meet challenges and overcome obstacles. These aren't training problems.

JAPANESE MANAGER

WHAT DOES IT TAKE to build productive employees and managers? The recipe is probably much the same in every country. It includes some combination of formal training, on-the-job learning, coaching, reinforcing performance that is on track, and redirecting it when it isn't. Everything in the mix is important. But Japanese and North American organizations often differ in how much emphasis they place on various aspects of developing employees. Differences are perhaps most apparent when it comes to training.

Japanese organizations often find that their understanding of the role and purpose of training is at odds with the expectations of North American employees, especially managers. One reason is that North Americans tend to view training as an "event," often conducted away from the workplace. These training events occur at predictable intervals in a person's career. Japanese organizations are more likely to consider training part of an ongoing development process. Coaching, on-the-job learning, and broad exposure to various aspects of the company—these are the principal elements of the process. Conspicuously absent are formal training programs conducted away from the immediate work environment. That's because training is not so much an event as part of the natural environment in which employees function.

There are also, of course, major differences in the skill levels that new employees bring to the job. Typically, firms in Japan assume that certain skills and knowledge will be present in most newly hired employees. North American firms must test for those skills and often provide remedial training.

One measure of the importance placed on training in North American organizations is apparent in the amount of money spent on training. A conservative estimate of U.S. and Canadian expenditures for outside training is nearly $43 billion annually.* When internal training costs are calculated, including the salaries of employees in training, North American organizations might spend several hundred billion dollars more. Where does the money go? Typically, into the following major categories of training employed by North American organizations:

• **Company-run training programs** build the specific skills needed for new assignments, new jobs, or the adoption of new processes and methods. This is by far the most common type of training. Programs can last a few hours to several weeks and are run by specialists from the company's training department or by assigned employees, especially line managers who have received training in training others. Training can take place at company training facilities or at hotels and business meeting facilities. The content and design of company-run training may be developed internally by the organization's training department or by specialized outside vendors who train company personnel to deliver programs.

• **Consultant-run training** is a vast business in North America, with thousands of large and small consulting companies and individ-

---

* *Training Magazine/Lakewood Research*. U.S. Training Industry Survey, 1991. Figures relate to companies with 100 or more employees.

ual consultants. It ranges from public seminars, open to anyone who pays a fee, to programs designed for specific companies. Consultants and consulting companies usually offer specialized expertise—from statistical process control to empowerment and team building. They save companies the expense of having training specialists on staff and offer unique skills and knowledge not necessarily available within the organization. Consultants also have a certain status as outside authorities, because in North America, as elsewhere, people tend to listen more closely to outside "experts" than to familiar inside figures.

• **University-sponsored programs** can range from half-day general overviews of current topics or trends to intensive weeks-long advanced management programs for senior executives. Many North American colleges and universities have discovered that business training is an enormous source of revenue and, therefore, have expanded their offerings far beyond MBA-type programs. The growth has been fueled by a trend among North American corporations to routinely send managers "back to school" at pivotal points in their careers, often when they are promoted or receive new assignments. These programs serve the purposes of updating the general management skills of managers, broadening their horizons in terms of organization design and function, giving them an international perspective, and so forth. Many of the managers attending these programs already have advanced degrees, but ten or twenty years might have passed since they graduated.

The prestige of university management development programs varies according to the reputations of the sponsoring institutions and the quality of the programs. Ivy League universities and other schools, such as Stanford University and the University of Chicago, attract senior executives from many Fortune 500 corporations. Regional and state institutions often serve executives from the surrounding business communities and middle-level executives from larger firms. In addition to exposing executives to the latest management thinking and top academic business theorists, university programs provide executives with valuable contacts among their peers at other organizations. Not surprisingly, such programs are attracting increasing numbers of Japanese executives—sent by their companies to gain an intimate perspective on the upper levels of North American industry.

ARE NORTH AMERICANS OBSESSED WITH TRAINING?

Motorola, the U.S. microchip and electronics manufacturer and Malcolm Baldrige National Quality Award winner, likes to boast that its employees spend more than 10 percent of their time in off-site training programs. Some of that training takes place at "Motorola University," located at the company's Illinois headquarters. IBM reportedly spends $1 billion a year on employee education and training. While Motorola's and IBM's commitment to formal training is high, it's not unusual for large North American companies to spend substantial amounts of money each year on training.

Typically, a manager at one of these training-committed companies attends as many as a dozen formal development programs during his or her working career. The training "transcript" of such a manager might look like this:

Introduction to Supervision (3 days)
Leadership Skills (10 weeks; 4 hours per week)
Interviewing and Selection (3 days)
Time Management (1 day)
Planning (2 days)
Advanced Leadership (3 days)
Training Skills (5 days)
Empowerment (2 days)
Presentation Skills (2 days)
Team-building Experience (3 days)
Accounting for Nonaccountants (1 day)
Developing Organizational Talent (2 days)
Delegation and Control (1 day)
Advanced Management Program (5 weeks at a university)
Retirement Planning
Many other programs in specific fields

To Japanese observers, this might seem like an obsession with formal training, but there is a logic behind the emphasis North American companies and their employees place on formal and regular training programs. The relatively narrow job experiences of many internal and external applicants often mean that active training and development programs, at all levels, are necessary to prepare managers for new jobs. A manager coming into a new organization, or a manager assuming a new position within his or her current organization, is expected to perform immediately. If a skill is missing, a formal training program is a quick fix for the problem.

THE JAPANESE APPROACH

The experience of Japanese managers can be very different. As we've seen, individuals in Japanese companies are "developed" by frequent new assignments, on-the-job learning in various company units and departments, and a methodical process of assimilating values and methods. The organization has plenty of time to get these things done, because job hopping is rare. This patient, methodical approach to accumulating experience is based on a common language and shared cultural experience, as well as years of living and breathing the company's vision and values.

Problems arise in Japanese organizations in North America because the same conditions rarely exist, at least in the short term. The exposure of North American managers to various aspects of the organization is much more limited. There is seldom time to take a slow, methodical approach to developing the talents of individuals. The kind of aggressive training and development programs that are beyond the historical experience of many Japanese organizations are usually needed.

NORTH AMERICAN EXPECTATIONS

Japanese organizations in North America have discovered that North American managers *expect* their employers to provide formal training and development programs because training is virtually a formal rite of passage into management positions in many large North American organizations. The "special event" quality of management training and the recognition it implies of an individual's value and potential further enhance its importance.

Thus, the presence of development opportunities makes a major contribution to job satisfaction among many North Americans. North Americans are less likely than the Japanese to assume that the organization is acting in their best interests, that "somebody is looking after them." With their more egocentric job orientation, they need evidence that the organization is providing opportunities for them to grow professionally and increase their value. In addition to meaningful job assignments, these opportunities are provided most clearly by training and development programs tied to a formal career development plan established by employees in collaboration with their managers.

In the past, career plans had a strong hierarchical orientation. They made clear the steps up the organizational ladder and showed managers how to prepare for them. Increasingly, career development plans are being called personal "learning plans" and are based on general, rather than specific, career opportunities. As corporate bureaucracies shrink and management layers are reduced, organizations are finding it increasingly difficult to lay out precise career programs for newly hired college graduates or incoming middle managers. They can, however, define the skills, knowledge, and experiences required by organizational levels and help an individual develop a plan to obtain them. The purpose remains the same: giving individuals a planned program to increase their skills and their value to the organization—as well as their professional value on the open job market.

Without such development opportunities, North American managers might feel trapped in what they perceive as dead-end jobs—a complaint frequently heard in Japanese organizations in North America. Ironically, many North American managers join Japanese organizations because they hold the promise of new and exciting learning opportunities. Instead, Japanese organizations can be very frustrating for the North Americans who join them, due to the lack of emphasis on explicit career planning, a relative lack of emphasis on management skills training, little perceived horizontal mobility, and the career advancement ceiling that North Americans feel they face. Eventually, the initial enthusiasm of North Americans may give way to disenchantment. The result can be high management turnover.

Formal training will not eliminate *all* of the frustration of North American managers, but it's a start. It is an important symbol of the organization's concern and a way to meet deeply felt personal growth needs. We feel it would be highly appropriate and advisable for Japanese and North American managers to attend training programs together to enhance team building and develop a core of shared concepts and skills.

A MIX OF ON-THE-JOB AND FORMAL TRAINING

But first we suggest that Japanese organizations take a close look at their training practices and carefully consider how applicable they are to North American settings. Some will be very appropriate, and others will need to be changed. An example of the differences between Japanese and North American approaches to training comes from comparing how organizations teach frontline employees statistical process control (SPC). In Japanese companies in North America, SPC is taught during team meetings. A team member, who has received special training, or the team leader provides a basic conceptual background, but the sessions rely heavily on coaching the team through multiple, real-life applications. Learning comes from actually doing. The team practices the methodology, receives feedback, tries again, and receives additional coaching.

In North American organizations, employees might be taken off the job for several days of classroom training. The trainers, who are often line managers, have been trained for one or two weeks in both "platform" training skills and SPC. Due to the classroom format, trainees often don't have an immediate opportunity to apply the skills learned and may not receive positive developmental coaching or feedback on their progress. While information is presented, real skills may not be acquired. In this example, employees in Japanese companies gain a lot more from the training because they have the opportunity to immediately practice skills in meaningful, real-life situations.

While on-the-job skill development—the Japanese approach— works best in many areas, it is ineffective in others. Many technical skills, such as math and blueprint reading, are better taught in a classroom setting, where both practice and feedback can be provided. Behavioral skills development is another good example. Managers often have a difficult time describing appropriate interpersonal behaviors to subordinate managers or supervisors. Experience has shown them how to handle a particular situation, but they have a hard time putting it into words. They might say, "You ought to be sensitive to the person," or "You need to coach the person," but that doesn't communicate the concrete steps that should be taken.

An even greater disadvantage is that it is difficult for subordinates to actually observe an effective model of how to handle such a situation on the job. Most managers would not allow their subordinates to observe them handling a difficult interaction with another subordinate because it would embarrass both parties. Finally, and most important, opportunities for practice and feedback are highly restricted in most on-the-job situations. A higher-level manager seldom is asked by a lower-level supervisor to sit in on a performance problem discussion with one of the supervisor's subordinates. Thus, the supervisor has no opportunity for feedback about what he or she said or did in the interaction.

An effective classroom training experience overcomes these problems. In classroom training, supervisors or managers can be given step-by-step descriptions of appropriate leadership or management behavior. These steps may be the result of considerable research and are presented in terms that are easy to understand. In many programs trainees can view a video of a manager effectively using the steps to handle a situation and then discuss how the video model used the steps. Finally, trainees practice holding discussions with one another in small groups and receive feedback on how well they followed the steps in their discussion. Such role-play situations in a "safe" and reinforcing classroom setting are effective in transferring the skills and the confidence to use them on the job.

Obviously, there is not one best way to develop talent. Sometimes on-the-job development is best, sometimes the classroom setting is best, and most often a combination of both is most appropriate.

Another difference between Japanese and American organizations lies in basic assumptions about trainer skills. Japanese organizations tend to assume that anyone who is capable of performing a task is capable of training others in it. North American organizations spend much more money on professional training design (content and how the training is presented) and in development of trainer skills. These skills are usually provided through formal train-the-trainer programs.

In theory a technically capable person can communicate his or her skills to others, but often it does not work in practice. Good athletes, for example, often are poor coaches. Some people are naturally proficient in a procedure or task but don't know how to present their knowledge or skill in a way others can understand.

We are not in any way implying that Japanese organizations must abandon their traditional training methods. Just the opposite—we feel they are very effective *for some skills.* The high skill level of Japanese employees in both Japan and the United States attests to that. We do, however, suggest that Japanese companies need to widen their repertoire of training and delivery methods especially for skills that can't be taught effectively on the job.

We think they'll discover that investing time and effort in planning and delivering training is a wise investment. There is the added benefit of everyone being trained in the same methodology or procedures, which is an advantage as organizations become more technologically complex and individuals are moved from one job to another.

WHO NEEDS WHAT? COMPARING TRAINING NEEDS IN JAPANESE AND NORTH AMERICAN COMPANIES

Technical Knowledge and Skills: Employees in Japan and North America need considerable technical knowledge and skill training. The difference is in how it is provided. Most Japanese companies excel in teaching technical knowledge and skills. For entry-level positions, tasks are well articulated and step-by-step procedures abound. Japanese coaches (often fellow employees) patiently help individuals learn each step required in a task. Typically, if a task involves multiple steps, the Japanese coach will first teach individuals the simple steps and then intervene to handle the more difficult steps. As the individual gains confidence, he or she is encouraged to tackle the more difficult steps. The coach stays with the individual until all steps in a particular skill cluster are learned.

North American companies generally are not as proficient at developing technical knowledge and skills. They often rely on designated trainers rather than those close to the job to provide training and coaching. The Japanese practice a philosophy of "tell them how it should be done, show them how it should be done, and let them practice while I watch." The Japanese coach provides constant performance feedback and suggestions until the trainee has developed the
continued

required skill level. North Americans might neglect the practice or feedback part of the skill development cycle. Unfortunately, for North American companies, practice without some kind of feedback needlessly extends training time. But as U.S. and Canadian companies become increasingly concerned about quality and productivity, many of them are adopting a more Japanese approach that uses more on-the-job practicing, coaching, and feedback.

Basic Computation, Manipulation of Data: Japanese firms generally assume that new Japanese employees are competent in numerical computation and the manipulation of data and often provide little training in these areas. In North America, "innumeracy" (as a lack of basic math skills has been called) afflicts even college graduates. Thus, remedial training in these areas is a priority in many North American companies. Training is usually provided in after-work classroom settings by professional trainers.

Communication Skills: Similarly, Japanese companies generally assume new employees possess basic oral and written communication skills. In North America, these skills can't be taken for granted, especially as increasing numbers of new employees who speak English only as a second language enter the job market. Thus, written and oral communication skills training becomes increasingly important in North American companies. Formal after-work classes are provided.

Oral presentation training is already common in North America. Few managers bring high levels of presentation skills to their jobs. When their job requires such skills, they usually have to be developed through some type of outside, formal training program.

While oral presentation training is not nearly as common in Japan, interest is growing as Japanese managers and executives increasingly spend more time communicating in multinational environments. A number of U.S. consulting firms specializing in this area have opened offices in Japan.

Interpersonal Skills: Most Japanese firms don't believe that people need training in how to get along with others, how to resolve interpersonal conflicts, how to influence others, or other people skills. Many North American firms feel just the opposite. They believe that skill levels in these areas vary widely and that the vast majority of North American employees and new supervisors and managers need some enhancement of interpersonal skills. Furthermore, they believe the best

continued

methodology for this kind of training is an off-the-job, more formal training experience.

Problem-Solving Skills: Companies in Japan tend to assume that employees have certain problem-solving skills but also work very hard teaching their own unique problem-solving methodologies. More important, managers consistently model the problem-solving methodologies and reinforce their use. Managers expect subordinates to follow these methodologies before presenting ideas. These methodologies form the foundation for continuous productivity and quality improvement discussions. *Kaizen* is both a value and a system with well-defined procedures.

The use of a prescribed problem-solving methodology that can be explicitly reinforced is much less common in North America, although increasingly practiced by the more progressive companies. In Japan the methodology is usually transferred in written form and by on-the-job coaching, but in North America it is more often presented initially in an off-the-job training program. The strength of Japanese companies is that they do an excellent job of creating the expectation that these methodologies will be used by all employees. The expectation that the problem-solving methodology will be used is not as explicit in many North American companies. Because of the lack of perceived organizational commitment to continuous improvement, employees often don't see the importance of the problem-solving methodology.

Leadership Skills: Typically, Japanese firms don't teach leadership. They assume that supervisors and managers have it or will learn it through watching others or from their own mistakes. North American companies feel that leadership is a group of learned skills and that it is more cost effective to teach people these skills before (or shortly after) putting them into leadership jobs. Thus, new leaders will learn from their successes rather than their failures, which is unquestionably a more effective way to learn. Typically, individuals promoted into leadership roles for the first time in North America (a new first-level supervisor, for example) go through at least one week of leadership training. As individuals progress up the managerial ladder, they might receive additional training relevant to their new leadership challenges.

Management Skills: Management skills include planning and organizing, delegation, and management control. Neither North American nor Japanese firms are particularly effective in teaching these skills,

continued

although North American companies provide far more formal training in these areas than do Japanese companies. Real skill development, however, is quite rare in North America, while it's almost nonexistent in Japan. In both countries, the philosophy apparently is that these things will be learned by watching one's superiors or through experience.

More progressive American companies, however, have developed excellent skill-building programs in these areas that all managers go through soon after their entry into management. The more effective programs relate the skills to practical day-to-day situations and provide ample practice opportunities during the training programs.

Company Vision (Mission) and Values: Japanese organizations (in Japan at least) more successfully communicate their vision and values to employees than do North American organizations. They do this through the use of frequent communications and symbols, modeling, and subtle reinforcements. In the past ten or fifteen years, many North American organizations have made attempts to instill in employees clear vision and values as a way to enhance empowerment and organizational focus and commitment. Japanese and North American companies tend not to reinforce their vision and values in a formal way, although new or revised vision (mission) and values statements are often introduced to employees with great fanfare. This might include the use of videos and workshops in which employees are gathered in groups to discuss the new mission and values and relate them to their particular job functions.

Company Organization: In Japan, individuals get a broad view of various parts of the organization through frequent job rotations and reassignments. During the course of a career, managers might go from production to finance to personnel to marketing. As a result, employees develop a fairly complete picture of how the parts of the organization fit together. In North America, managers tend to remain in specialized areas. Thus, North American companies often must provide orientation programs that explain how different parts of the organization function. New employees from outside the organization also need some way to understand the organization as a whole and develop contacts within other functions.

International Economics: This is a priority for Japanese and North American companies. Failing to provide an international perspective is one of the many inadequacies of the U.S. educational system. To

continued

compensate, many U.S. companies inject a heavy dose of training in international economics into management development programs. U.S. and Canadian companies also are including much more information on the laws and business practices of other countries in their development programs. The Japanese educational system is not much better than the United States in this regard. Thus, Japanese companies must provide formal training in business conditions and practices throughout the world.

17

GETTING READY FOR ASSIGNMENTS IN NORTH AMERICA

There is, of course, a great fascination with America and all things American in Japan. You think you know all about Americans. Then you get here and wonder if you really know anything at all.

JAPANESE MANAGER

Japanese managers approach training themselves with the same thoroughness they approach doing the job. The trouble is, not enough of them seem to get the kind of training they need.

AMERICAN MANAGER

THE TRUTHS ABOUT TRAINING

MUCH OF THIS BOOK has concentrated on the problems facing Japanese managers in Canada and the United States. In this section, we turn briefly to training solutions that can help Japanese managers tackle these problems. But first, it is important to describe some basic axioms or truths we've learned in more than two decades of helping organizations develop their human resources. These axioms form a foundation for the training model we suggest.

Our experience includes more than twenty years of working with Japanese organizations in Japan through the Management Service Center. We also have worked directly with large numbers of Japanese organizations in North America, Europe, Australia, and Southeast Asia. Based on this experience, we believe these axioms apply equally well on both sides of the Pacific.

1. **Know what you are trying to achieve.** In a management development system, an organization might want to (a) help an individual develop skills to be more effective at some task or responsibility (e.g., leading a meeting, programming a computer); (b) help an individual obtain knowledge (e.g., local laws or technical information); or (c) motivate an individual to take on new challenges or adopt new ways of working.

All three goals are important. The problem is that organizations tend to think they are doing one, while actually they are doing another. Frequently, organizations think they are developing skills when in reality they are providing knowledge about how to do something— not the actual skills to do it. For Japanese managers, the implication is that merely reading books, listening to tapes, or hearing lectures will not provide the necessary behavioral skills to be effective managers in North America. These methods provide useful knowledge, but they will not necessarily change behavior.

We believe the best method of developing behavioral skills is an approach called behavior modeling. Briefly, behavior modeling teaches managers interpersonal skills in much the same way that people are effectively taught technical skills. First, specific, effective behavioral steps are discussed with participants in a training session. Second, participants view a positive model video showing a manager following these steps in an interaction. Third, each participant practices the steps in a similar situation and then receives feedback. Through multiple repetitions of the sequence, managers gain the skills and confidence needed to handle a variety of job situations.

The training environment is constructed so that managers learn through a series of successes. Participants receive coaching before each practice session to ensure success. With each effective handling of an interaction, the participants' confidence is enhanced. The atmosphere of the training program is upbeat and supportive.

Many organizations try to change behavior by changing attitudes. This might be characterized as "preaching someone into being more effective." This approach seldom works because merely changing attitudes usually does not change behavior. Changing behavior *does* change attitudes, however. That is, if managers acquire both new skills and use the skills in a series of successful on-the-job experiences, their attitudes toward using those skills will change for the better. Thus, programs that effectively create an empowering workplace don't stop at explaining the virtues of empowerment; they teach the skills of empowerment *and* provide an opportunity for on-the-job application. The trainees notice the positive impact and change their attitudes.

2. **Rely on a combination of classroom training and on-the-job coaching and reinforcement.** As discussed in the last chapter, the leadership skills of typical Japanese managers usually are not developed in classroom situations but are developed principally through on-the-job modeling, coaching, and reinforcement. Japanese managers observe the behavior of effective managers and copy it. Then they receive feedback on their behavior (although often it's extremely indirect) from senior managers.

This approach has several limitations when used as a method of developing leadership and management skills. In addition to being time-consuming, it relies on skilled senior managers to be appropriate models and to provide subordinates with feedback on performance. This doesn't always work because skills vary from manager to manager, and some are better models than others. The greatest limitation is that this approach requires learners to sense which behaviors make the manager effective, rather than having it clearly spelled out. This experience is similar to trying to learn baseball without someone explaining the game's subtleties and nuances. You can learn eventually, but the process is lengthy and inefficient.

We believe that for managers to learn effective interactive and management skills, the best combination is classroom training that uses behavior modeling to teach the basic skills, followed by on-the-job practice with feedback and reinforcement from *their* managers, who have been trained in the same skills learned by their subordinates, and who themselves model the use of those skills consistently and systematically.

3. **Integrate training activities so that training experiences reinforce each other.** Time and training effectiveness often are lost due to confusion caused by changes in terminology, conceptual models, and procedures among training programs. For example, a participant might go through two training experiences to develop leadership skills, but those training experiences might use different words to describe leadership behaviors, might be based on different conceptual models of human interaction, and might use markedly different training methods. The participant in the second program has to determine how the new material fits into what he or she has previously learned. These incompatibility problems are compounded by the language difficulties experienced by many Japanese. It is hard enough to learn many of these concepts without needless complications.

The ideal training system has closely interlocking parts that build on concepts from the other components, allowing the learner to experience a continuous growth cycle.

Developing a truly integrated development system is management's responsibility and requires the coordination of everyone who provides input.

4. **Provide training when it is needed.** Motivation to learn new skills or knowledge is heightened when people know the new skills will be needed soon. Also, the less time that elapses between learning a skill and the opportunity to perform it and receive feedback, the greater the chance that the learning will stick. For instance, a manager with a report due tomorrow will be highly motivated to learn the new computer spreadsheet program needed to complete the report. Similarly, Japanese managers are much more motivated to learn conversational English when they face a North American assignment than when they were in school.

Often, Japanese managers coming to North America are hit with a barrage of training programs during an intensive two- to three-week "crash course" in Japan before starting their assignments. While these programs are better than nothing, they require managers to learn too many new skills too fast and too soon. Before the information or skill can be applied, much will have been forgotten.

Because training should occur as close as possible to when the skill will be used on the job, initial training for Japanese personnel coming to North America should focus on tasks that will be required early in their new assignments. An example is a new manager facing an immediate need for different communication patterns (saying "yes" and "no" unequivocally, making direct requests, providing feedback and praise). The manager might be asked to comment on the vision and values of the organization in ways that are relevant to local employees and, undoubtedly, will be involved in meetings. The skills that will be needed quickly should become training priorities.

Later, training can become more sophisticated as English skills improve and Japanese managers begin assuming new responsibilities. Hiring new employees, conducting performance management discussions with subordinate managers, and making formal presentations and speeches are skills that Japanese managers might need later—and all are heavily dependent on being fluent in English. This is why our development plan suggests communication/leadership training first, followed by a series of short courses on more advanced skills.

5. **Consider individual needs when designing training programs.** Not everyone needs training in everything. In fact, some Japanese candidates already will have many of the skills needed for success in North America. Effective training takes these individual differences into consideration. After the initial training, from which everyone can benefit, we recommend that an individualized development plan be constructed.

Tailoring training to individuals requires an accurate assessment of individual needs. In North America, three methods generally are used: (1) evaluations by superiors, (2) diagnostic assessment centers (in which individuals are observed as they participate in simulations of job-related situations [see box]), and (3) peer and subordinate feedback (often involving the use of questionnaires).

While the first two methods are routine in Japan, the third—asking employees to rate managers—might strike employees and managers as a wildly inappropriate idea. In recent years, however, this type of assessment has gained popularity in North America, and we see no reason why it can't be as beneficial to Japanese managers as it is to North American managers. Using this approach, a manager distributes questionnaires to five or more key subordinates or colleagues and

DIAGNOSTIC ASSESSMENT CENTER USING VIDEOTAPE TO RECORD BEHAVIOR

More than 100 Japanese companies in Japan use some form of the Assessment Center Method to diagnose training needs. In Japan, managers go through a series of job simulations that require them to work in groups, solve problems, make decisions, and so forth. They are observed and evaluated by other managers being assessed and by consultants. Pooling the observations, the consultants prepare a lengthy report that includes developmental recommendations.

The U.S. and Canadian systems are similar, except higher-level managers are more often used as assessors (although increasingly consultants are used), and input from fellow assessees is unusual or nonexistent.

For nearly twenty years, Japanese companies have videotaped participant behavior in the simulations to provide the participants with an opportunity to assess themselves. This technology has been expanded in the United States by doing all the assessment via videotape. Participants' behavior in the simulations is captured on videotape and assessed by highly trained assessors at a different time and location. Many of the largest U.S. organizations have used this technology. Its big advantage is its cost—between $500 and $700 per assessment. Another advantage is the availability of a large number of national norm groups that candidates can be evaluated against. A company can choose one or more appropriate norm groups to serve as the basis for comparison. Thus, a manager who is assessed can see how he or she stacks up against people at the same managerial level with similar education. The results can be highly motivating.

fills out one himself. The questionnaire asks respondents to rate the manager on various behaviorally defined dimensions related to job success. Responses are anonymous and, after being tabulated by a computer, are given to the manager along with appropriate developmental suggestions. The perceptions and evaluations of subordinates and other co-workers are used to help the manager define his or her individual training needs. This technique can be a powerful motivator as well. If managers know they are seen by subordinates and peers as performing poorly in certain job dimensions, those judgments can stimulate improvement.

If an organization wants to adopt a diagnostic-prescriptive model of training, it needs a method by which to diagnose ongoing training needs. While the judgment of higher-level managers is important, we recommend this feedback be supplemented by other types of insights, such as the peer and subordinate feedback just described, or a diagnostic assessment center.

6. **Schedule training in small pieces.** Compare an hour-long tennis lesson once a week for five weeks (with plenty of practice between lessons) with five hours of tennis lessons all at once. Which would make you a better tennis player? Most people would say that the lessons distributed over the five-week period would be more effective than five consecutive hours of lessons.

The same is true for some types of training. In North America, many skill-building programs for first-level employees and supervisors are designed in two- to four-hour modules so that they can be conducted in segments—usually once a week. Managerial programs typically are designed in one- to three-day segments. Between segments, individuals have an opportunity to practice the skills they are learning and receive feedback.

Our development plan contains both concentrated and distributed training. Sometimes concentrated training is more cost effective. But when we prescribe a week or more of such training, we suggest introducing a range of subject matter to keep the training varied and interesting. Days of uninterrupted language training, for example, may not be very effective. In addition to producing fatigue, uninterrupted blocks of training offer little practice time and little chance for individuals with different learning styles to sift through what they have learned. We suggest that organizations intersperse language skills training with interactive skills training and provide no more than one-half day of language skills training per day.

7. **Make training relevant to the experiences of the trainee.** Too often, managerial training programs are variations of college classes in which a professor lectures to students. The assumption is that the professor knows everything and the trainees know nothing. A more effective methodology draws upon the knowledge and experiences of the trainees. It assumes that truths and insights can be discovered from shared experiences. Managerial training programs

should treat managers as adults who have earned their place in the world and who are ready to improve upon an already significant level of ability.

8. **Build self-esteem and confidence.** A good training program builds the self-esteem of trainees and gives them the confidence to apply new skills. Too many training programs result in a high degree of fear instead of a high level of skill and confidence. Self-esteem and confidence are enhanced when a trainee experiences success in class-room practice situations. This is achieved, at the start, by providing relatively easy practice opportunities, coaching learners between practice opportunities, and then increasing the difficulty as skill and confidence improve.

9. **Don't be fooled by titles.** Organizations do not buy expensive equipment without first making sure it does what it's supposed to do. This may not be true, however, when organizations choose training programs. They are fooled by impressive titles or the credentials of trainers and training consultants. They determine that the advertised training will meet their needs and pay less attention to the quality of the training.

To avoid expensive mistakes, organizations should carefully prede-termine their training needs, develop priorities based on those areas that are causing the most problems, and then seek programs that demonstrate effectiveness in the target areas. Corporate consumers of training should not hesitate to ask for proof of a program's training effectiveness. Validation should be in the form of proven behavioral or organizational changes, not in a "smile index" that purports to show how well people liked the program. The latter typically is unrelated to meaningful behavioral change or organizational improvement.

A MODEL DEVELOPMENT PLAN

To show how these "truths" can be put into practice, we present an example of a possible development plan for a Japanese mid-level manager about to embark on his (or rarely, her) first assignment in North America. (We assume a mid-level manager in his thirties who studied English in college but rarely had the opportunity to use it.) This manager might have visited North America as a tourist or on a research assignment but never for more than two or three weeks. His development needs are:

- English-language skills
- Leadership skills
- Presentation skills
- Performance management skills
- Delegation and control skills
- Developing organizational talent skills
- An understanding of the North American work environment and North American employees
- The ability to stay current on technical skills and knowledge

The following suggestions explain how these needs might be addressed.

Development Activity #1—English-language training combined with interaction skills and basic individual and meeting leadership skills. This program might involve a concentrated ten-day period, with one-half of each day spent in language training and one-half in behavioral skills and leadership training. In the latter, language skills could be reinforced in practice situations. For example, participants might be asked to prepare an informal speech in English for North American employees about the vision and values of their organization. Feedback would be provided on content and language skills. The effects of culturally based communication would be emphasized—for example, translating Japanese communication patterns into patterns that are clear to North Americans, and developing an understanding of how culture affects the way North Americans communicate. Videotaping would be used to provide feedback to trainees. (Ten days off-site in Japan)

Development Activity #2—English-language training combined with advanced leadership training, information on the EEOC, and other important laws. Because immersion is an excellent way to refine language skills, this program would be conducted totally in English in North America. (A Japanese translator or trainer would be present to help the trainees over the rough spots.) Approximately one-half of each day would focus on English skills, the other half on more advanced versions of the individual and group leadership and communication skills learned in Japan. Not only would English skills be enhanced but participants would also gain a better understanding of important legal issues facing Japanese companies in North America, particularly EEO laws.

Ideally, this training would take place before the individual reports for the first assignment. (Twelve days off-site in North America, including one weekend used as an "adventure in American living" with visits to private homes, etc.)

Development Activity #3—Ongoing English tutoring. Depending on the skills of the individual, we recommend at least one or two hours per week of tutoring for the first year. In addition to a business focus, this tutoring might focus on a North American hobby or avocation. Developing an in-depth knowledge of some key aspect of North American culture and life (professional sports, politics, music, arts, etc.) is one way for Japanese managers to forge a common interest with North Americans. (One to two hours per week on-site)

Development Activity #4—Interviewer training. Training in interviewing skills can reinforce many of the issues addressed in EEO law. Developing interviewing skills will enable Japanese managers to begin working closely with their North American counterparts in making important selection and promotion decisions. Such training can develop behavior evaluation skills that can be expanded on in subsequent performance management training. (Three days off-site)

Development Activity #5—Performance management training. Japanese managers need to know how to help subordinates set key result areas and objectives and how to coach subordinates and conduct performance appraisal discussions. This training needs to be tailored to the system used by the Japanese company and needs to focus on developing behavioral skills. (Three days off-site)

Development Activity #6—Delegation and control training. This program would deal with the more advanced skills of defining roles effectively, empowering delegation, and setting up control systems that provide the information needed by the Japanese manager and organization, while not *un*empowering the subordinate. (Three days off-site)

Development Activity #7—Advanced "diversity" orientation. Because of the cultural and ethnic diversity of North American employees, Japanese managers need to continually broaden their understanding. Speakers, seminars, exercises, and other activities can be used to deepen the Japanese manager's insights into the effects of diversity in the workplace. The emphasis should be on understanding how the behaviors of managers should be adapted to fit the special needs and viewpoints of different groups, including women and minorities. Courses should be tailored to the makeup of the company's work force and the local community. (One day each year for three years off-site)

Development Activity #8—Civic involvement. In addition to formal diversity programs, we suggest that Japanese managers participate in at least one civic activity in their North American communities. Japanese managers will discover dozens of opportunities—from Chambers of Commerce and Rotary Clubs to numerous civic and community development groups.

Increasingly, Japanese organizations are making major financial contributions to cultural and civic groups in their communities. Philanthropy is seen as one of the obligations of a concerned corporate citizen, but there are other ways to demonstrate a sense of responsibility. In addition to cash contributions, the technical and management insights and skills of Japanese managers would be welcomed by many groups that seek the business community's participation on boards, task forces, and committees.

There are several valuable aspects to this type of participation, not the least of which is the service Japanese managers can provide to local communities. In addition, participation in community groups offers Japanese managers greater opportunities to increase their communication skills and develop insights into community life—away from the pressures and tensions of the workplace. Japanese managers will discover that their colleagues in these groups will greatly appreciate their participation, will be intensely curious about their lives and reactions to North America, and will be tolerant of language and other communication problems. Needless to say, participation in community groups is also a good way to make North American friends outside the work environment.

Perhaps most important, visible and enthusiastic participation by Japanese managers in community groups is one of the best ways to demonstrate that Japanese organizations, far from being aloof and exploitative, take their responsibilities seriously as major employers in local communities.

Development Activity #9—Developing organizational talent training. This area includes the skills needed to diagnose the developmental needs of North American managers and to take appropriate action. It also would provide skill training in on-the-job reinforcement of skills that subordinates have learned in training and development activities. The training also would make the Japanese managers more effective in developing subordinate Japanese managers and workers. (Two days off-site)

Development Activity #10—Advanced presentation skills training. Skill development in this program would cover making effective presentations in large meetings and to outside groups. This course would be geared to Japanese managers with good English-language skills. (Two days off-site)

(Activities 4 through 10 would be provided on an "as-needed" basis during the first two years of the manager's assignment.)

Development Activity #11—Attendance at professional and technical meetings. Japanese managers should become involved in professional and technical groups related to their specialties. One way this can be accomplished is by attending at least one technical program in a specialty area per year—not only to stay current on technical information but also to become acquainted with peers in other organizations.

Development Activity #12—University-sponsored training programs. For Japanese managers who have lived in the United States for more than three years or who are on a second assignment, attending a one-week university-sponsored training program on an appropriate topic is advised. In addition to the program content, university programs introduce Japanese managers to their peers from other organizations and provide insights on "how things really operate" in North America.

Development Activity #13—Study groups. Many North Americans working in Japan belong to study or discussion groups that let them share their insights and experiences in dealing with the Japanese. We know of no comparable formal study groups for the Japanese living in North America, but they might be happening informally. Study groups could be supported by Japanese companies. They would work best if the members came from different organizations so that discussions could steer clear of technical issues.

INVOLVING SPOUSES

A male Japanese manager's adjustment to North America will be greatly influenced by the experiences of his wife. Our observations suggest that the acculturation of a manager's wife is almost completely dependent on her comfort level with the English language. Active efforts must be made to help Japanese wives develop their English skills. Japanese wives also will need help adjusting to different social affairs in North America. One of the biggest cultural differences is that company and community social events in North America often involve wives and family members. The faster a spouse becomes comfortable with North Americans in social settings, the more comfortable the manager will feel. We suggest that Japanese organizations follow the lead of other multinationals in encouraging and supporting the language and cultural skills development of their managers' spouses. Currently, many Japanese organizations offer a one-half- or one-day program for wives going overseas. This does not seem to be nearly enough and needs to be enhanced with training once the wives are in the United States or Canada.

Japanese children, like children everywhere, show a great deal of cultural flexibility. They usually find it easy to adapt to the new rhythms of North American society. If anything, Japanese parents worry about their children becoming too "Americanized" during North American assignments. The problems encountered by Japanese children often are the opposite of the problems facing their parents: Instead of trying to learn how to function smoothly in North American society, Japanese children spend time learning how to retain their essential Japanese character.

18

DEVELOPING NORTH AMERICANS TO SHARE CONTROL

There is no career planning here, no obvious place to go.

U.S. MANAGER

Come work for a Japanese company if you're looking for an interesting experience, but don't stay too long.

U.S. MANAGER

They keep us long enough to learn what we know. Americans are a disposable commodity with them.

U.S. MARKETING EXECUTIVE IN CALIFORNIA NOW SUING HIS FORMER JAPANESE EMPLOYER

THE NATIONAL ORIGIN PROBLEM

THE GROUNDS FOR the last manager's legal suit are becoming familiar to many Japanese organizations in North America. The American complains that his former employer, a giant electronics manufacturer, has systematically discriminated against North American employees. As proof, he points to the fact that the company has fired hundreds of American employees over the past five years, but has never dismissed a Japanese employee.

During the layoffs, the American claims, local managers and employees were given generous severance packages and told that, because of the market and economic circumstances, there was no longer a place for them within the company. But somehow there was always a place for Japanese employees, who were reassigned to other operations or to jobs back in Japan. When this American lost his job last year, he claimed he was fired because it was simply time for a Japanese manager to be rotated into his position, a high-level marketing job. The American had laid the groundwork. Now a true "company man" could take over.

The American's suit prompted an investigation by the EEOC, which found that the Japanese manager who replaced him had less experience and education and, compared head-to-head, appeared less qualified.* There were several other key differences the EEOC didn't explore. The Japanese manager had come to work for the company right out of college and expected to continue working for the company until retirement. His new position was just one of a string of similar developmental assignments he had held in the company. His reassignment was normal for someone from the right school, who had the right allies within the organization, and who was obviously on the inside track to a top-management position.

The American, on the other hand, was a veteran of a half dozen California companies. He didn't speak Japanese, had not been carefully brought up in the company's culture, and did not understand how the company hierarchy operated. Advancement for any manager would have required eventual reassignment to a position in Tokyo. For

* Kilbourn, P. T. "U.S. Managers Claim Job Bias by the Japanese." *New York Times*, June 1, 1990, p. A1.

an outsider like the American, such a possibility seemed remote. The company simply wasn't designed to be run by people like him. He would have stuck out like a sore thumb.

Similar complaints about discrimination by Japanese subsidiaries are being heard throughout North America. In Illinois, three American managers complained that layoffs at a large Japanese television manufacturing facility included sixty-six American managers, but no Japanese managers. A federal court penalized the company more than $2 million.* In the early nineties, large Japanese companies, including Sumitomo and NEC, settled similar suits alleging discrimination based on national origin.† Many more suits are expected as the nineties continue. While large Japanese companies are discovering they have to pay close attention to the issue of national origin discrimination, smaller, less sophisticated Japanese companies as well are discovering that employing North Americans is sometimes a minefield. As the head of JETRO, the influential Japanese organization that promotes U.S. trade, told *The New York Times*, "We admit that the number of Americans in management is quite limited. Japanese companies like to keep management the Japanese way."‡

IS THE JAPANESE WAY THE ONLY WAY?

The "Japanese way," based on a common tradition and approach to business shared by few who haven't been brought up in the system, is often cited as the most significant reason for the exclusive nature of Japanese management. The organizational dynamics of Japanese companies are unique, both Japanese and Western observers say. You reach for "through-the-looking-glass metaphors," one American business professor said after researching differences between Japanese and Western business. Japanese practices, "if not always the

---

* Kilbourn, P. T. "U.S. Managers Claim Job Bias by the Japanese." *New York Times*, June 1, 1990, p. A1.

† Galen, M., and L. Nathans. " 'White People, Black People' Not Wanted Here?" *Business Week*, July 10, 1989, p. 31.

‡ Kilbourn, P. T. "U.S. Managers Claim Job Bias by the Japanese." *New York Times*, June 1, 1990, p. A12.

reverse, are at least substantially different from conventional U.S. approaches."*

The few statistics available make it clear that Japanese firms are far more uncomfortable with giving local managers authority than other multinationals. Figures from Japan's Ministry of Trade and International Industry show that only about 30 percent of top positions in Japanese subsidiaries in the United States are held by local executives. Many in this group undoubtedly hold relatively little decision-making authority compared to managers with similar titles in North American companies. Figures for Japanese subsidiaries of North American and European multinationals tell a different story. Those companies fill 80 percent of their top slots with Japanese managers, although as we've seen, the complaints of Japanese managers working for foreign companies often mirror those heard in North America.†

The incompatibility of non-Japanese managers in Japanese organizations is very real, but it is not impervious to change. The question is: Can this situation last indefinitely? In addition to its long-range implications relative to global competition, the cap on advancement opportunities for North Americans in Japanese companies—a very real "*gaijin* ceiling"—puts companies on a collision course with local expectations and with local employment laws. Japanese companies simply can't imply that certain jobs are closed to non-Japanese employees, although this might provide North American employees with a more realistic assessment of their career potential in Japanese companies. As these lawsuits and government actions show, such a message would be in open defiance of North American employment laws and social standards. Yet, the behavior of many Japanese companies is sending virtually the same message.

TAKING A LONG-RANGE VIEW

Many of the problems facing Japanese companies in North America arise from what we feel is a short-term view of employee development. Few seem willing to invest the same amount of time and effort

* Camillus, J., J. Grant, and D. Slevin. "Through the Looking Glass." *Managing Magazine,* January 1991, pp. 10–12.

† *Fortune Magazine,* December 30, 1991, p. 120.

in developing North American managers as they do Japanese managers. Of course, there are a few exceptions: Consider the experiences of David Warren, age thirty-two, a vice-president of corporate planning in Sumitomo Trust & Banking Company in New York, described in *Business Tokyo Magazine* (June 1990):

> Warren majored in Japanese as an undergraduate at Brigham Young University, hit what he felt was a "limited ceiling" in a job at Mitsui Manufacturers Bank in Los Angeles, and went on for a Harvard MBA in 1987. From Cambridge, with lots of encouragement from a Japanese classmate who had studied at Harvard under the Sumitomo aegis, Warren signed on with the bank. Warren's way in: an experimental program under which he was considered a local hire in Japan. After two years in Tokyo, he was reassigned to New York, and after a three- to five-year tour here, he was to go back to Japan for a time. As a Tokyo-hired employee, Warren was offered the prospect of lifetime employment—a luxury even many Japanese cannot claim. Just as important, he has far more "access to information and corporate policy" than employees hired in the United States.

According to *Business Tokyo Magazine,* Sumitomo has sent other young American managers to Tokyo. Usually these managers are housed in company dormitories. They receive the same modest salaries as other company "freshmen," and work the same twelve- to fourteen-hour days. The company says they are "blank sheets," and is waiting to see what kind of "Sumitomo men" they become after they are absorbed and processed by company culture. Honda is another company trying out an experimental exchange program between North American and Japanese workers. In recent years, Honda has sent more than forty American supervisors and managers to Tokyo on assignments lasting up to three years. Before being assigned, the Americans spent six months learning Japanese language and customs.*

Most North American managers, however, have little realistic prospect of being sent to headquarters. A summary of hypotheses explaining the reticence of Japanese companies to invest in the long-term development of non-Japanese managers might look like this:

---

* Jacobs, D. L. "Japanese American Cultural Clash." *New York Times,* September 1, 1990, sec. 3, p. 25.

1. It is difficult to find foreigners who will learn Japanese and make the necessary sacrifices expected of a Japanese management trainee.

2. North American managers are temperamentally unsuited to fit into the top-management, decision-making structure of Japanese companies and could never manage a Japanese firm as well as Japanese managers.

3. Japanese organizations, no matter how far-flung their operations, have tight, hierarchical control. This control is not shared easily with outsiders.

4. North Americans are not long-term players in the Japanese sense. They don't make permanent, lifetime commitments to employers, so why should Japanese employers do so, especially when it might require substantial structural changes? For the same reason, investing in the training and development of non-Japanese managers can be risky and even foolish. Why invest heavily in employees who might bolt the company when a better opportunity comes along?

The first three reasons reflect attitudes that probably cannot be changed by extolling the skills and commitment of North American managers or management trainees. Legal action might have temporary effects on Japanese employers, but it probably won't make long-term changes in deeply held attitudes. These attitudes, however, *can* be changed through positive experiences. Those experiences will occur when more Japanese organizations experiment with the concept of "growing their own people" in North America.

The most successful North American and European multinationals have gone through the same learning cycle that Japanese companies are experiencing now. This is particularly true with American organizations. As they expanded overseas operations and subsidiaries, American companies reflected the same lack of trust in local employees as Japanese companies do today. But enough experiments with decentralized management proved that locally hired managers could do an equal or better job of running operations because of their knowledge of the local conditions. Eventually, what had been experimental became routine.

None of this is intended to make it sound easy. Because of the cultural gulf between Japan and most of the rest of the world, the evolution of Japanese companies into integrated, multinationally run organizations will be difficult. But the transition has to be made. In an age of instant communications and global marketing, organizations whose parts are at odds with themselves will eventually run into trouble. Better integrated competitors will be able to respond to market changes faster.

The ability to hire talented local managers who will *stay* with the organization is one of the biggest challenges facing Japanese companies. The high management turnover rate, endemic in the North American job market, is a familiar and depressing story to many Japanese companies. Such turnover invariably complicates the job of developing local management trainees and makes it far costlier than developing Japanese trainees. In some North American organizations, only one out of five newly hired management trainees is still on the payroll after ten years.

Improved selection systems can attack the turnover problem. Because a job with a Japanese company is highly coveted in North America, Japanese companies have excellent selection ratios (applicants per job opening). This gives companies the opportunity to choose employees carefully and get the most out of hiring investments. In addition to assessing the usual management skills, the proper selection techniques can evaluate the ability of local candidates to learn Japanese and to adapt to Japanese culture and management practices.

Admittedly, the issue of learning the Japanese language is controversial. Few Japanese companies in North America have pushed it, but it's clear that the linking pins between Japan and North America have to be bilingual. As long as the only bilingual people within a company are Japanese, long-range development opportunities for North Americans will be limited. At the very least, the communication gap virtually assures that Japanese subsidiaries will be headed by Japanese executives, whether it's officially acknowledged or not. There is a great need to find North Americans who can speak Japanese or, more realistically, who can learn it. Because finding management talent with good Japanese-language skills is difficult in North America, a development plan that includes Japanese-language training as part of managers' growth within the company might be a more sound strategy.

Japanese organizations should be realistic about the ability of North Americans to learn Japanese. We estimate that less than 20 percent of adult managers have the ability to learn a language as complicated as Japanese. Fortunately, this aptitude can be predicted with various psychological instruments. When used as part of the selection process for management trainees, Japanese organizations can learn who has the needed combination of management skills and language-aptitude skills.

In addition to emphasizing bilingualism, Japanese organizations need to make other major changes. Many Japanese companies seem unwilling to invest in developing female employees, no matter how highly educated, motivated, or bilingual they are, because the Japanese feel that between the ages of twenty-six and thirty, these women will marry and leave the work force to raise a family. That pattern is changing in Japan and has long been obsolete in North America, where career women are a fact of life. Companies that want to get the most out of their work forces must be particularly cognizant of providing equal opportunities for all trainees—male and female. Many North American companies are encouraging females with high potential to continue working through marriage and motherhood by providing day-care centers; babysitting services; flexible, nontraditional work schedules; maternal and paternal leaves; and other benefits and programs that allow individuals to balance careers and parental obligations.

One advantage Japanese companies have in North America is that many are relatively new and represent to many local employees a clean break from the past. Because they start from scratch, Japanese organizations can become leaders in EEO, quality of work life, and family initiatives. Benchmarking the practices of progressive North American organizations is one good method for developing programs and policies that will establish Japanese organizations as leaders. Several Japanese automobile manufacturers, because of their visibility and the controversy surrounding their entry into local labor markets, have been especially aggressive in this area, and their efforts have clearly paid off in employee satisfaction as well as productivity that surpasses U.S. automobile manufacturers.

The expanded role of women in the North American work force is just one of several differences that Japanese companies should consider as they develop ways to integrate North American trainees into their emerging global organizations. Japanese organizations need to define the dimensions (behaviors and knowledge) that are required for job success at senior levels; then they should determine the most efficient way to develop them. As organizations and technologies become more complex, the list of dimensions needed by senior managers grows. This forces organizations to seek new and innovative development methods.

We recently went through such an exercise with a large Japanese organization. We listed the dimensions for senior management, the job assignments necessary to master each dimension, and an estimate of the time a manager should serve in each assignment before moving on to the next one. When we added up the times, we concluded that fifty years of development would be required to produce a senior manager! Obviously, a faster method of acquiring skills and knowledge is required.

Rotational job assignments are an excellent method of development, but there are many other alternatives, including formal training programs, interactive video, and self-study. In addition, job assignments can be organized so that more skills and knowledge are acquired in a shorter period of time. One retail organization reduced the time needed for a management trainee to reach the department manager level from five years to two years to one year. This was done by clearly specifying what the trainee had to learn in each assignment; providing extensive written technical and operational information; and by training store managers in training, coaching, and support skills. The company reduced management costs substantially. More important, it boosted the motivation and productivity of North American trainees, who saw that they could assume decision-making and supervisory responsibilities relatively quickly.

Viewing North American business school graduates as "blank sheets" and sending them to Japan to live in company dormitories, receiving salaries that are little more than cost-of-living stipends, as in Sumitomo's case, is a genuinely radical approach. It might guarantee that relatively few North Americans will want to become "Sumitomo men" because of the perceived hardships involved. Sumitomo and other multinationals might do better to look for ways to develop more innovative development methodologies that combine the best of the traditional approaches in building company loyalty, teaching company values, and orienting trainees to company operations, with new approaches that build skills and knowledge more rapidly. They might try to balance classroom experience and other methodologies with job assignments that instill the traditional fraternal values that have made companies like Sumitomo so prosperous.

That's not to say many North Americans aren't willing to sacrifice to fit into Japanese organizations. Nissan recently opened a research and development center near Detroit and managed to recruit several hundred local automotive engineers from nearby U.S. automakers. It was a challenge, the company's top American engineering official reported, because Nissan requires all new engineers, regardless of experience, to begin by performing the most basic and mundane design chores as part of the process of learning its design philosophy. Engineers who might have worked on important mechanical components at Ford or General Motors were asked to design door handles and glove compartments for Nissan.* Their long-term satisfaction will depend, of course, on the levels of responsibility Nissan eventually gives them, but it is significant that so many applied, knowing that Nissan was essentially asking them to start over.

These American engineers represent only a handful of the many thousands of North Americans who have been willing to break with the past by joining Japanese organizations. Thousands more will join Japanese companies in the years ahead. Despite the occasional negative story reported in the North American press, the chance to be part of some of the most successful and technologically innovative organizations in the world is still an opportunity that is irresistible to many individuals across North America. However, as things stand now, many North Americans will continue to find the experience frustrating and disappointing; some will find satisfaction in Japanese organizations; and a few will thrive and ultimately become thoroughly integrated into the culture of their employers. The challenge is to change the ratio of these three groups and afford Japanese organizations the full benefits of a talented, motivated North American work force.

---

* Maskery, Ann. "Management Mysteries." *Automotive News,* May 28, 1990, p. 6.

19

BREAKING THE SHOGUNATE

This is a little-known recent side effect to U.S.-Japanese indus-
trial competition. Even as some American manufacturers de-
mand more protection from Japanese rivals, U.S. companies are
looking to the Japanese not just as potential customers but as
help-seekers. Sometimes the complainers and the help-seekers
are the same people. . . . A growing number of little companies
. . . are trying to learn from the Japanese, too. The result is a
quiet, company-by-company revitalization of U.S. industry.

Wall Street Journal,
September 9, 1991, p. 1

PREDICTING THE FUTURE of something as vast and complex as
Japanese-North American relationships in the workplace poses obvious risks. A decade ago, few could have predicted the depth and
strength of Japanese organizations in Kentucky, Ohio, the Carolinas,
Washington, Oregon, Southern California, Ontario, and numerous
other places. Although few can predict with much certainty how those
organizations will function a decade from now, a safe assumption is
that Japanese subsidiaries will be different.

One possible scenario: Japanese subsidiaries now dominated by
Japanese managers, receiving daily orders from Japanese headquar-

ters, will have evolved into more decentralized operations that rely to a great extent on the judgment and decisions of locally hired managers and employees. The Shogun syndrome, with Japanese personnel acting as aloof *"samurai"* administrators relaying orders from a distant seat of power in Japan, will be a fast-fading memory. Instead, Japanese and North American managers will be partners in running their organizations. The organizations will represent a new, "blended" alternative to historical Japanese and North American organizations. These new organizations will possess strengths that transcend the older organizations they supplant. And, most likely, they will be uniquely positioned to thrive in the marketplace conditions of the next century.

A less sanguine scenario sees the conditions described in this book steadily deteriorating to the point that the very viability of many Japanese subsidiaries in North America is threatened. Evidence of the dissatisfaction of a substantial percentage of local managers is quite apparent. As managers continue to perceive Japanese limitations on *"gaijin"* managers as unfair, turnover certainly will become a prominent issue. The training and knowledge invested in these managers will be wasted. Management continuity, already a problem in Japanese subsidiaries in North America, will be difficult (if not impossible) to establish as successive generations of Japanese managers are "rotated in" to overcome the problems of ineffectual local management. And truly effective management—management that can use local resources productively and respond quickly and flexibly to changing local conditions, as well as operate in a global context—might never develop.

Other side effects of the lack of progress toward truly integrating North Americans into Japanese organizations are easy to predict. The suspicion and acrimony that exist in a minor way in Japanese-North American relationships today will escalate. Charges of unfair employment practices, discrimination, and racism will increase. Legal challenges will mount. At the employee level, the blush of enthusiasm caused by working for new and very different Japanese organizations will fade quickly. The lack of consistent, understandable, empowered, and *sympathetic* local management inevitably will have an effect on labor-management relations. The issue of empowerment will become critical. As empowerment becomes the accepted method of capturing the commitment and loyalty of employees in North America, the limited empowerment in Japanese organizations could pose a major handicap. The surest route to empowering employees is to empower their managers and supervisors. But that remains perhaps the biggest stumbling block for Japanese organizations in North America, which continue to follow—at least in many North American eyes—the Shogun model.

One thing is clear: During the eighties, the tables were turned on North America, especially the United States. During those years, Japanese companies came to North America as investors, employers, and, surprisingly, as *teachers*. In fact, some of the same Japanese executives who toured the United States after World War II to learn how to rebuild Japanese industry returned to the United States in the seventies and eighties to rebuild North American industry along Japanese lines. And now, North American companies are learning many lessons from working with Japanese companies—sometimes reluctantly, but the process is unfolding inevitably. And after North American companies learn enough from the Japanese to *compete* with them, then what?

BEYOND THE SHOGUNATE: BRINGING THE OUTSIDERS IN

The major challenge to Japanese organizations, as we've suggested, is changing the perception and the reality of the North American manager's experience in Japanese subsidiaries. The perception: Working for a Japanese company represents a kind of vassalage, albeit a lucrative one. "They want your hands, not your heart," is how one American hotel executive puts it. By that, he means that while North Americans are hired because they have needed skills, few perceive that the organization can or will afford long-term career opportunities to outsiders.

Some Japanese subsidiaries in North America are offering a different, much more hopeful reality to North Americans. These organizations have what a North American human resources specialist might call a strong people orientation. Despite production efficiencies focusing on low-cost and high-quality products, the companies are at heart very low-tech. They depend heavily on employee involvement—not computers, robots, and machines—to meet production targets and keep quality high. When the clash of cultures threatens to block efforts to work together harmoniously, these companies are adept at improvising solutions. The key seems to be the freedom local Japanese managers have to make decisions without undue interference, control, and second guessing from headquarters. In turn, Japanese managers are able to transfer some of this trust and authority to local managers, who feel relatively empowered to make decisions on their own, rather than passively waiting to be told what to do.

Other Japanese organizations reflect profoundly different orientations. Companies with a strong engineering/technological focus, often expressed in rigid production philosophies, have management and human resources practices that seem less successful in coping with cultural differences. People matter less than procedures. These organizations tend to have high employee-turnover rates in North America. Turnover, however, appears to be acceptable as long as the production system can accommodate it, which it is designed to do. Among managers, relationships tend to be rigid. Rules and systems are tightly defined. There is little room for initiative. When cultural misunderstanding or conflict arises, situations tend to fester because the organization lacks the flexibility to go beyond the rules and devise alternative ways of working.

The primary difference between the two types of organizations is the level of confidence and trust that organizations have in local, non-Japanese managers. Without confidence and trust, many Japanese companies only partially empower local employees and managers. For these companies, certain types of control and decision-making authority always will be off limits to North Americans. Advancement beyond a certain level will be impossible. Japanese managers on the scene will continue to be perceived as mysterious and autocratic. These companies can degenerate into a parody of the effective Japanese organization—one that observes all the forms but lacks the substance. The substance, of course, is employees with a deep sense of commitment and identification.

REDUCING JAPANESE PRESENCE AND TRUSTING LOCAL MANAGERS

With better methods of recruiting and developing local managers, and a commitment to decentralized operations, Japanese organizations might discover that control problems solve themselves. Giving local managers more control can be approached in numerous ways, as some Japanese companies have shown. Often it involves encouraging local managers to communicate with decision makers at headquarters instead of through coordinators and advisors.

An important way to build trust is to establish and adhere to a timetable for the withdrawal of coordinators and advisors. This does not mean, however, that "withdrawn" advisors won't be returned to North America; they likely will be if management turnover or other problems arise. But the implicit offer of control that many North American managers seem to believe they were given when they joined Japanese companies should be observed. That is, local managers should be developed systematically to take over from their Japanese advisors and run the operation within the limits defined by the corporation.

Clearly, the only way to do this is by placing more emphasis on developing North American managers for positions of increasing responsibility within Japanese organizations. This will require more attention to formal career development and learning plans than is typical of Japanese organizations. Before that can happen, the first step for many Japanese organizations will be defining what career development *means* for North American managers, and what experiences and requirements managers need in a blended Japanese-North American organization. We've also seen that career planning, training, and development play important roles in satisfying the personal continuous learning expectations of North Americans, and that without them North American managers feel trapped in dead-end jobs. For this reason alone, Japanese companies should invest more in human resources development programs.

A major component of the career development of North Americans should be programs to increase understanding of Japanese culture and, more specifically, Japanese business culture. Whenever possible, Japanese-language training should be emphasized—not to create fluent Japanese communicators out of average North Americans, but rather to sensitize North Americans to the difficulties faced by the Japanese when communicating in English. The training should encourage both sides to develop alternative, innovative ways to build a common basis for understanding. Of course, a few North Americans will discover an aptitude for learning and speaking Japanese. North Americans who truly want to excel in Japanese will make the effort, arduous as it might be. Sometimes, all they need is encouragement and motivation, which few Japanese organizations currently provide.

By all means, Japanese organizations should send North American managers and key employee groups to Japan. These trips prove extremely insightful for those North Americans currently fortunate enough to make them. Of course, these trips need to include explicit learning objectives. Too often managers now feel like tourists and are not sure what they are to gain from the experience.

DEVELOPING BILINGUAL MANAGERS FOR THE LONG TERM

Because people at the highest decision-making levels in Japanese organizations in North America inevitably must speak Japanese and English, it is essential that Japanese organizations start to develop North Americans who can assume these roles in the future. This will involve practicing the same systematic methods of developing managers in North America that is practiced in Japan, starting with recruiting recent college graduates who show enthusiasm for long-term careers in Japanese organizations.

It would be a mistake to select North American managers *only* on their fluency with the Japanese language. Management skills are critical as well. We believe the best long-term approach is to recruit management trainees (through rigorous interviewing and testing processes) who have the ability and the motivation to learn Japanese *and* the potential to become effective leaders. Of course, once they are hired, these individuals' training should involve assignments in both cultures.

PREPARING JAPANESE MANAGERS FOR THEIR ROLES IN NORTH AMERICA

Many of the problems that arise in Japanese subsidiaries in North America can be traced to the inadequate English of Japanese managers, their inadequate understanding of North American culture, and inappropriate assumptions about North Americans. Fortunately, these problems can be overcome with a greater investment in training. We believe that Japanese assigned to management positions in North America would be far more effective with the type of classroom training we have already outlined. This greater effectiveness would have an impact on their success in North America and on their entire careers. An intensive program aimed at understanding and managing people as different as North Americans would give Japanese managers the tools and the insight to prepare for assignments in other foreign markets, which will play an increasingly important role in the plans of many Japanese companies in the years ahead. We have found, for instance, that the four key principles we have described have led to management successes throughout Europe, Africa, and most of Asia.

Moreover, by investing in leadership and management training for Japanese personnel, Japanese companies will develop a core of multinational management specialists—as many U.S. and European global companies have—and will be able to move them around as needed. With this type of Japanese personnel—flexible, culturally savvy, effective in communicating, attuned to the needs and nuances of managing foreign work forces—Japanese companies will avoid many of the "teething" problems that figure so prominently in North America today.

Japanese companies are very willing to invest in many types of training, but some have been relatively unwilling to invest in managerial training of the very people in whose hands the concept of a blended organization rests. As we've seen, without this training, Japanese managers can be clumsy in their relationships with North American managers and supervisors. It's clearly time for a change.

A FINAL WORD ABOUT NORTH AMERICANS

Our main focus has been the challenges facing Japanese organizations in adapting to North American conditions. But it would be a mistake to conclude that the burden of change rests solely with the Japanese. In many areas, North Americans need to change far more to achieve a blending of Japanese and North American talents.

While North Americans might complain that Japanese organizations are culturally monolithic and inflexible, North Americans can seem just as unyielding and set in their ways to Japanese managers. In a Japanese organization in North America, when both sides are convinced that their traditional organizational patterns, management systems, and values are superior, a kind of unhealthy status quo mentality develops that prevents the organization from evolving. Japanese managers might conclude that building the organization means simply waiting for North Americans to come around to the "right" way of thinking and acting. North Americans, meanwhile, can become convinced that the Japanese will have to become more "American" before progress is made.

In many organizations, the higher up you go, the more common this attitude becomes. When it comes to Japanese and North American managers and executives, values and traditions are often so entrenched that a blending of talents often seems impossible without aggressive efforts to force change. While it is important for Japanese organizations to question the relevance of purely Japanese management practices in North America, it will be just as important to recruit and hire North Americans who are willing to question their own assumptions, behaviors, and expectations as well. North Americans who join Japanese organizations bring strongly held beliefs that are dictated by education, culture, and previous job experiences. When these "traditional" North Americans meet the Japanese organization, the results are often predictable—on the North American side, resentment over limited development opportunities, impatience with a poorly understood decision-making process, and a perception of a "*gaijin* ceiling" that limits advancement; on the Japanese side, perceptions that local managers are chronic complainers, lack patience and analytical skills, and are impulsive and self-centered.

We've already identified some of the changes North Americans need to make to erase these perceptions. For starters, North Americans need more realistic expectations about their potential in Japanese organizations and, if a long-term career is desired, a more realistic appreciation of what building this career might require. One requirement could be the ongoing study of Japanese language, business culture, and management philosophy. North Americans also might need to reevaluate their feelings about compensation and personal rewards, the role and authority of managers, and how planning is accomplished and decisions are made. Japanese organizations should help local managers make adjustments through training in management-level and executive-level teamwork, consensus planning, and decision making.

An important objective for any North American manager hoping to build a career in a Japanese organization is experience with the parent firm in Japan or other operations and subsidiaries. We've already said that it is important for Japanese organizations to make these experiences a routine part of developing promising North American managers. But it is also essential that North American managers vigorously prepare themselves to take advantage of these experiences, which means that North American managers might have to become quite aggressive about language and communication training. They also will have to acquire a good understanding of how the parent company and Japanese businesses operate. Much of this learning will have to be pursued on the local manager's own initiative, which is similar to how Japanese managers develop themselves. This will require hard work and sacrifice—more so, perhaps, than most jobs with North American organizations. That again is part of entering Japanese organizations with realistic expectations.

Our experience suggests that North Americans will need to be more assertive about getting the kind of career development opportunities they feel they need. North Americans should understand that many Japanese organizations historically have different ways of training and developing people. If these methods seem inadequate to the demands of North America, it is up to North Americans to lobby for change within Japanese organizations. Because Japanese managers are both uncomfortable and unfamiliar with Western-style performance feedback and appraisal methods, it could be unrealistic to expect them to take the lead in blending Western and Japanese methods.

North Americans should understand that information and communication flows differently within Japanese organizations. Not everything they think they need to know will be clear-cut and explicit or handed to them on a routine basis. Basic communication also can be difficult because of language and cultural differences. Innovative and resourceful responses to communication challenges will be required of North Americans who hope to find satisfaction in Japanese organizations.

Japanese organizations can't change North American managers, but North American managers can change themselves. While the organization can encourage their transformation through training and development opportunities, the mind-set and motivation needed for North Americans to thrive in Japanese organizations must come from within. Careful recruiting through testing and assessment, especially of managers early in their careers, can identify North Americans who have the potential to succeed in Japanese organizations. New forms of management development programs can greatly increase the odds of their success. The ultimate goal should be devoting the same attention and care to developing North American managers that is now being devoted to developing Japanese managers. This is the bottom-line requirement for a truly blended Japanese-North American organization.

CONFIDENCE IN THE FUTURE

The experiences of successful Japanese organizations in North America suggest the workplace values that need to be emphasized: trust, communication, sensitivity to the personal and family situations of employees, and a willingness to provide opportunities for non-Japanese managers to advance and assume increasing responsibility. We are confident that these necessary changes are fully within the capabilities of Japanese organizations. Indeed, some of the challenges seem minor compared to the challenges that Japanese organizations have already overcome.

As they learn from experience, many Japanese organizations are evolving slowly into blended, global organizations. It is, in some ways, a natural and unstoppable process.

The message of this book is that a greater sense of urgency is needed. We hope some of the ideas we've presented will help Japanese organizations quicken the pace. A strong, innovative partnership is the goal of many Japanese organizations in North America. First, we must cut through a fog of miscommunication and cultural differences. The time to start is now.

GLOSSARY OF
JAPANESE TERMS

Bucho (Bu-chō) Head of department

Gaijin (Gai-jēēn) Any non-Japanese person

Gaijin ceiling (Gai-jēēn) The perceived limits placed on upward mobility of foreigners in Japanese companies

Honne to Tatemae (Hōn-nay; Tă-tă-mă-ā) True intention vs. Official stance

Kacho (Kă-chō) Section chief, work group manager, and other middle managers

Kaizen (Kī-zĕn) Continuous improvement

Kakaricho (Kă-kă-rē-chō) Entry-level manager

Kuuki (Kū-ki) Air or atmosphere

Muda (Moo-dă) Fruitless, futile

Nemawashi (Nā-mă-wă-she) Consensus decision making and preliminary negotiation methods

Omoiyari (Ō-mō-ē-yă-rē) Consideration of others and their feelings

Shainn (Shă-ēn)   Employee

Tsuikiai (Tsū-kē-ăe)   Meeting after office hours in bars/
restaurants to carry on a combination
of business and social activities

Ura to Omote   Hidden implication vs. Superficial
(Oo-ră; ōmō-tay)   dialogue

Wa (Wă)   Social harmony

JAPANESE ORGANIZATIONAL HIERARCHY

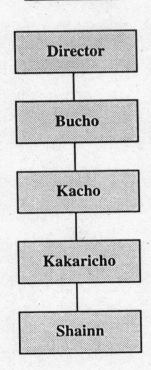

OTHER BOOKS BY
WILLIAM C. BYHAM, Ph.D.

Zapp! The Lightning of Empowerment with Jeff Cox

Zapp! in Education with Jeff Cox and Kathy Harper Shomo

*Empowered Teams: Creating Self-Directed Work Groups
That Improve Quality, Productivity, and Participation*
with Richard S. Wellins and Jeanne M. Wilson

Assessment Centers and Managerial Performance
with George C. Thornton III

For more information about these books, write or call:

Development Dimensions International, Inc.
World Headquarters—Pittsburgh
1225 Washington Pike
Bridgeville, PA 15017-2838
800/933-4624

A WORD ABOUT
DEVELOPMENT DIMENSIONS
INTERNATIONAL, INC.

DEVELOPMENT DIMENSIONS INTERNATIONAL, INC. (DDI), is a leading provider of human resources programs and services designed to create high-involvement organizations. Its activities fall into three primary areas—organizational change, assessment and selection, and training and development. Its numerous training programs are designed to provide managers, supervisors, and employees with the skills necessary to make high-involvement and empowerment a reality within their organizations.

DDI has more than twenty years of experience consulting with Japanese companies in Japan and North America. DDI is proud to have maintained close, ongoing partnership relationships with many major Japanese employers.

DDI's World Headquarters and distribution facilities are located in Pittsburgh, Pennsylvania. It maintains offices around the world, including North American training centers in New York, Chicago, Los Angeles, Atlanta, Dallas, Denver, Toronto, and Montreal.

For more information about Development Dimensions International and its products and services, please call our Marketing Information Center at 800/933-4463.

INDEX

ABOUT THE AUTHOR

WILLIAM C. BYHAM is president and chief executive officer of Development Dimensions International, Inc. (DDI), a multinational human resources firm that offers integrated training programs and services, emphasizing supervision and management skills, personnel assessment and selection, and multilevel strategies for quality and productivity. DDI has offices in major cities worldwide, with 7,000 active clients and programs in twenty-two languages. Prior to cofounding DDI in 1970, Byham was manager of Selection, Appraisal, and General Management Development at the J. C. Penney Company, and assistant to the executive vice-president of a New York City advertising agency.

Byham, who earned a Ph.D. in industrial/organizational psychology from Purdue University, is recognized as one of the outstanding thinkers in the areas of selection, training, and human resources development. He has written more than 100 books, monographs, and articles. In recognition of his achievements, he has received more than a dozen professional awards, including the highest professional awards given by the Society of Industrial and Organizational Psychology and the American Society for Training and Development.

For more than twenty years, Byham has researched and written about how to create an empowering culture—particularly in the area of developing the behavioral skills of employees, supervisors, and managers who want to be empowered or to empower others. His book *Zapp! The Lightning of Empowerment* has sold more than one million copies and is available in nine languages. Byham consults on both empowerment and management selection and development issues with leading organizations throughout the world, including many Japanese organizations.

A frequent visitor to Japan, Byham and his colleague, Dr. Douglas Bray, were responsible for introducing the assessment center method of employee skills diagnosis as well as behavior modeling skill development techniques in Japan.